THE SECOND BATTLE
OF THE ALAMO

THE SECOND BATTLE
OF THE
ALAMO

How
Two Women
Saved Texas's
Most Famous
Landmark

JUDY ALTER
BASED ON THE RESEARCH OF
DEBRA L. WINEGARTEN

TWODOT®

Helena, Montana
Guilford, Connecticut

A · TWODOT® · BOOK

An imprint and registered trademark of The Rowman & Littlefield Publishing Group, Inc.
4501 Forbes Blvd., Ste. 200
Lanham, MD 20706
www.rowman.com

Distributed by NATIONAL BOOK NETWORK

British Library Cataloguing in Publication Information available

Library of Congress Cataloging-in-Publication Data available

ISBN 978-1-4930-3131-3 (hardcover)
ISBN 978-1-4930-3132-0 (e-book)

∞™ The paper used in this publication meets the minimum requirements of American National Standard for Information Sciences—Permanence of Paper for Printed Library Materials, ANSI/NISO Z39.48-1992.

For Texas Women
And in memory of
Debra L. Winegarten

CONTENTS

———•◦•———

Interior of the Alamo chapel. Adina Emilia De Zavala Papers, The Dolph Briscoe Center for American History, The University of Texas at Austin.

ACKNOWLEDGMENTS

This is Debra Winegarten's book. Always has been. She conceived the idea, wrote and presented the proposal, secured both an editor's interest and a contract. She accumulated boxes, and I mean that literally, of books, photocopies of documents and pictures—a wealth of research material. I only met Debra once but felt like I knew her well through a small and close-knit online writers' group we both belonged to.

A woman of incredible energy, she was an author, a publisher with her own company, Sociosights Press, a public speaker in high demand, and an educator. She was fiercely proud of being a Texan, a feminist, gay, and Jewish. She went to all sort of meetings, because she could—and did—network, coming away with new invitations to speak and ideas for books. I thought of her as the Energizer Bunny come to life, with a piercing sense of humor. She went out of her way to help others. A woman in our writers' group was overwhelmed by the prospect of selling her book at a professional meeting in California. At her own expense, Debra flew to California and staffed the sales booth, so the other woman could schmooze.

Probably the most important thing Debra taught us was the magic of the outrageous request—because she found she usually got what she wanted when she made such a request. One O.R., as we called them, on her part, brought about my long study of the second Battle of the Alamo. I knew she was working on the book, and when she got deeply involved in her other projects, Susan Wittig Albert and I would try to nudge her back to the Alamo book. My personal interest in it sprang from a long career writing about women in Texas and the American West, and I was delighted for Deb that she had this project.

In July 2018 Debra was diagnosed with metastatic lung cancer. She'd been plagued in recent months by health issues which seemed mild—a paralyzed vocal cord, an extremely painful hip. But she and her heart partner and wife, Cindy Huyser, were unprepared for the devastating diagnosis. Debra was immediately hospitalized, and her hospital room became a community gathering place. She gathered minyans in the chapel, she arranged for a twentieth anniversary celebration for her hand-fasting with Cindy, complete with lavish buffet, she dispensed books freely, she was the hostess par excellence from her hospital bed—but she did not respond to treatment.

Debra called me one day, which was a surprise, because ours was not the kind of relationship that required such personal communication. When I asked what I could do for her, she croaked in her whispery voice, "Write the Alamo book." I agreed immediately, and she sent her outrageous request to the editor requesting that the contract be transferred to me.

Debra L. Winegarten died September 10, 2018, seemingly at peace with her world.

Debra's notes included her intended dedication of the book, and I think it appropriate to repeat that here:

To Nancy Baker-Jones, Janelle Dupont, Theresa Cost, Melissa Hield, Cynthia Beeman, and Kay Reed Arnold, of the Ruthe Winegarten Memorial Foundation for Women in Texas History, whose work keeps alive the stories of Texas women.
And the memory and legacy of my beloved mother, Ruthe Winegarten

Thanks go to Cindy Huyser who packaged all of Debra's books and other research materials and had them delivered to me. Cindy, a talented and award-winning poet in her own right, is executor of Debra's estate, so we keep in touch about various matters. In addition, she's someone I've come to like and admire a great deal.

And endless gratitude goes to Erin Turner, editor at Rowman & Littlefield, who allowed us to make the change in authors with alacrity. From my first tentative letter to her, Erin has been encouraging and wonderfully helpful. Her critiques are positive, with suggestions that lead me in new directions for improving the manuscript. Working with her has been a joy.

Thanks, too, to Bob Brinkman of the Texas Historical Commission, who went to the trouble of asking his staff to run down an obscure bit of historical fact for me.

Finally, thanks to family and friends who listened patiently every time I burst with excitement over a new and obscure piece of Alamo history.

"Dawn at the Alamo." This 1905 painting is the best-known work by San Antonio artist Henry Arthur McArdle. A student of Texas history, he relied on documents, photographs, maps, and personal reflections to create this iconic painting. It did not sell during his lifetime but was later purchased by the State of Texas and hung in the State Capitol Building. When the original painting was destroyed in the 1881 fire that leveled the capitol building, McArdle painted another version. Today it hangs in the Senate Chamber of the Texas State Capitol Building. Library of Congress.

INTRODUCTION

---•●•---

A BIT OF TEXAS HISTORY, OR
WHY THIS STORY MATTERS

"Remember the Alamo!" Those three words have echoed across the nearly two centuries since Sam Houston invoked them in his defeat of Mexican General Santa Anna at the Battle of San Jacinto. Generations of Texans learned those words practically in the cradle, and tales of the heroic fight for Texas independence are required reading in schools across the Lone Star State. Texas children have played "defending the Alamo." They pretend to be the valiant Texians in homage to their fallen heroes, bravely fighting off an overwhelming Mexican Army as their little bodies collapse in heaps. Texas parents routinely take their young children to see the sacred mission in San Antonio. It's part of growing up in Texas. And the battle cry is universally recognized around the world as unique to Texas and a symbol of freedom.

In the early nineteenth century, Americans continually pushed the frontier westward after declaring and winning independence from Great Britain. Looking for new frontiers to conquer and civilize, Anglo settlers displaced native peoples and carved farms and settlements from what had been the wild frontier. These Americans believed that the destiny of the new nation was to expand to the Pacific Ocean, exploring the seemingly boundless territory and exploiting its natural resources, making useful farmland out of the wilderness. Americans believed it was their obligation to create one huge, productive farmland across North America, from ocean to ocean. God, they often contended, did not mean for the land to be a wasteland. This widespread belief became known as Manifest Destiny.

Nowhere was the rush to settle and "civilize" the frontier more evident in the early nineteenth century than in the Mexican province of Coahuila y Texas, the northernmost region of Mexico, roughly covering the area that is now Texas and the northern part of present-day Mexico. Anglo settlers from the eastern United States had targeted this land for settlement both because of its suitability for farming and raising market animals and because they expected to be free from constraints by the government of Mexico in distant Mexico City—and possibly because they would also be far from the centralized government in Washington, D.C. At first, the Spanish government of Mexico welcomed the idea of Anglos' help in developing these heretofore ignored lands. The citizens of Mexico had been at war with their mother country since 1810, partially prompted by unrest in Europe and partly inspired by the revolutions in the United States and France. After more than ten years of conflict, Mexico gained its independence from Spain in 1821, and the newly installed government's policies included continuing to allow emigration. By 1836, the Mexican government had been issuing generous land grants to immigrants from the United States for more than a decade. These land-grant holders were known as *empresarios* (the Spanish word for businessmen).

In return for land, an *empresario* was obligated to bring a certain number of settlers with him to develop the land. The Anglo immigrants who followed *empresarios* to settle the land grants became known as Texians. Moses F. Austin was the first *empresario* to receive a grant for what was known as Austin Colony, and his son, Stephen F. Austin, known as the "Father of Texas," is the most famous of the *empresarios*, leading a group of settlers who came to be known as the Old 300 into the territory in 1823 and 1824. The Austin name, of course, designates the state capital today.

After its initial generosity and laissez-faire attitudes to the Texians, the Mexican government, determined to maintain control over their part of the new world after gaining its hard-fought independence, eventually sought stricter controls over the immigrants. Determined that the province remain essentially Mexican in language and culture, the government strengthened immigration laws to require of new settlers such things as belonging to the Catholic Church, speaking Spanish, having a craft or talent to contribute to the settlement, and checking with authorities for permission to settle. Perhaps unsurprisingly, given the grit and independence that would have led them to take on the challenge of settling the area, the settlers on these lands increasingly rebelled against these new laws and the heavy taxes imposed by Mexico. These, after all, were the very circumstances that had caused previous Anglo generations to revolt against Great Britain.

After years of unrest, in 1833 General Antonio López de Santa Anna became president of Mexico. Although Santa Anna had expressed a belief in democratic principles, after he was installed as president, he became—in fact—a military dictator. Since Mexico had gained its independence from Spain, interest from the United States in the region had increased. By the end of the 1820s, the number of colonies started by Americans was on the rise. And in 1827, President John Quincy Adams had made overtures to Mexico about buying Texas. As Mexico was going through its own growing pains—starting a new government, establishing leaders—the Texians began agitating for their independence. Further, when slavery was outlawed in Mexico, it was a blow to the primarily southern Texian immigrants. To Santa Anna, the Texian unrest in the northern state was a land grab by Texians and a rebellion against his newly formed government, and he was determined to put it down.

Santa Anna claimed Texians did not pay taxes; they countered that they got no services from the government. The Texians at first hoped to negotiate better terms with Mexico, but several emissaries sent to Mexico were imprisoned, and it became clear to the settlers that Mexico would not relent. Full independence became the Texian goal, and on March 2, 1836, Texas declared itself an independent republic. A constitutional convention was convened, and a constitution adopted on March 15.

There had been numerous skirmishes over the first few weeks of 1836 between the Texians, Americans recruited to support the Texas cause, and Santa Anna's army. After the political separation was declared by Texas but even before the constitution was adopted, Santa Anna marched north from Mexico City with several thousand men to quell what was now outright rebellion. He had no battle plan, no strategy, no plan for provisions for his men, no equipment, and his army included many untrained men that he swept along with him as he marched north. But he was armed with the vengeance and cruelty of a dictator.

Under the leadership of Sam Houston, the Texians cobbled together a ragtag army to defend the new republic against Santa Anna's troops. The San Antonio de Valero Mission, better known as the Alamo, a Catholic mission in what is now San Antonio, was a location crucial to the Texian defense since it sat on the main road from Mexico through the newly independent Republic of Texas. It was there at the mission, in the two-story long-barracks building near the already crumbling chapel, that the Texians made their defensive stand.

The newly installed governor of Texas, Henry Smith, had ordered Colonel William Barret Travis, a lawyer who had volunteered for the Texas army, to recruit one hundred men and move to the defense of San Antonio, reinforcing the men already gathered there to fight. Travis was only able to enlist twenty-nine men to join the Texian Army as regulars, but at the governor's insistence, he took those men to San Antonio and the Alamo, where about fifty men under the command of Colonel James Clinton Neill awaited his arrival. Hearing of the planned defense of the Alamo and the approach of Santa Anna's troops, famed frontiersman and soldier of fortune Davy Crockett arrived at the mission with a small group of volunteers. James Bowie, sick with fever, arrived with a hundred volunteers and ordered his men to report to Travis. Some of the volunteers were no doubt mercenaries and men looking for adventure but others were determined to fight specifically against Mexico and for Texas. Several other volunteers were Mexicans who had been living in Texas and who arrived to fight alongside Travis. Under Travis's command, the Alamo was fortified, stocked with provisions, and prepared for battle as much as the small army could manage. In spite of these defense measures, most Texians did not believe that Mexican troops would actually reach their settlements—until the advance army was visible from the towers of the church.

In late February, Santa Anna's troops, having taken possession of the city of San Antonio, began a thirteen-day siege of the Alamo complex. San Antonio was, at that time, the population center of Texas. Within the city, the buildings of the Alamo mission-turned-fort were a logical gathering place. Inside the fortification wall, the hastily cobbled-together supplies ran short; messengers risked their lives to leave and return to the barracks structure, bringing news of the other battles between Houston's army and Mexicans, along with reports on the declaration of the new republic. The massive force outside the walls of the mission meant that the men inside were virtual prisoners. Late one night, deep into the siege, Colonel Travis sat at a small desk, in a room illuminated only by flickering candlelight, and dipped his pen in ink. He wrote:

> *To the People of Texas & All Americans <u>in the World</u>:*
> *Fellow citizens & compatriots—I am besieged, by a thousand or more of the Mexicans under Santa Anna—I have sustained a continual Bombardment & cannonade for 24 hours & have not lost a man. The enemy has demanded a surrender at discretion,*

otherwise, the garrison are to be put to the sword, if the fort is taken—I have answered the demand with a cannon shot, & our flag still waves proudly from the walls. <u>I shall never surrender or retreat</u>. Then, I call on you in the name of Liberty, of patriotism & everything dear to the American character, to come to our aid, with all dispatch—The enemy is receiving reinforcements daily & will no doubt increase to three or four thousand in four or five days. If this call is neglected, I am determined to sustain myself as long as possible & die like a soldier who never forgets what is due to his own honor & that of his country—<u>Victory or Death</u>.

William Barret Travis
Lt. Col. comdt [sic]

P.S. The Lord is on our side—When the enemy appeared in sight we had not three bushels of corn—We have since found in deserted houses 80 or 90 bushels & got into the walls 20 or 30 head of Beeves.

This letter, now known at the "Victory or Death" letter, has been called one of the most patriotic letters in history. Colonel Travis's words sealed the fate of the men gathered at the Alamo.

On the night of March 5, Travis assembled his troops within the barracks, both regulars and volunteers. Slightly fewer than three hundred men stood *en masse*, waiting for him to speak. Slowly, he looked at them, studied them. Some few of the waiting men were in uniform, but most were in work clothes and were armed with whatever weapons they could bring to the fight. Travis knew these men were about to die. He saw bedridden Jim Bowie, of knife-wielding fame, and his own cousin, James Bonham, a young man who'd carried messages to and from the Alamo but could no longer penetrate the Mexican lines. And there was explorer and frontiersman Davy Crockett.

The men waited patiently for their leader's words. Finally, Travis drew his saber and, walking the length of the line, scratching a line in the dirt. "I ask all who will fight to the death with me to cross the line and stand by me."

One by one the men crossed the line to stand by Travis. Bowie asked that his sickbed be carried across the line. Only one soldier, a French volunteer named Louis Moses Rose, declined to stand and fight; he slipped out of the mission during the night and escaped into the darkness, stopping eventually at the home of W. P. and Mary Ann Zuber, where he spilled out his story. The Zubers later published their version of Rose's account.

Early on the morning of March 6, Mexican bugles shattered the air with "Deguello," the march tune that signals that no quarter will be given to the enemy. Santa Anna's vastly superior number attacked the long barracks. The entire battle probably lasted no longer than thirty minutes, and by mid-morning, all of the defenders of the Alamo were dead, their bodies burned. A couple of soldiers, deserters from the Mexican Army, were said to have survived by pretending to be captives of the Texians, and for some time after the battle various people claimed to have survived the slaughter. However, those reports were never confirmed. In the aftermath of the battle, some who entered the Alamo described the long barracks floor as "shoe-deep in blood."

A few women and children had been on site during the siege and had sheltered in the rooms at the north end of the chapel during the siege. This small group of survivors did not witness the battle. The most famous of the women survivors was Susanna Dickinson, whose husband was among the dead. Mrs. Dickinson had sheltered in the sacristy during the fight. She carried her infant daughter, Angelina, with her out of the chapel and would later claim that Santa Anna treated her with great courtesy as she was escorted to safety. The story is told that Santa Anna offered to adopt Angelina into a life of luxury, but the child's mother refused, steadfastly holding on to her infant. Angelina became known as the "Babe of the Alamo," and while she was still young, a Texas legislator proposed a resolution to provide funding for her education, but the bill failed to pass. Angelina married early, divorced, and left her children with her mother while she moved to New Orleans and came to no good end.

Another woman, Andrea Castañón Villanuevea, known as Madam Candelaria (her husband's first name), survived the siege and later claimed to have been in the Alamo nursing the bedridden James Bowie during the fight. Since she was the mother of four, raised twenty-two orphans, and was known for tending the sick, her story is plausible. Historians have never verified her presence at the Alamo, but neither have they completely discounted the story. She held fast to her account of events until she died in 1899 at the age of 113.

Fictionalized representation of the Battle of the Alamo by Percy Moran. Note the woman kneeling at a man's knee. No women were present during the battle. Library of Congress.

After the defeat of the Texians at the Alamo, General Sam Houston, commander of the Texian Army, did not attack Santa Anna's troops. Instead, he led his ragtag army east, away from the Mexican Army. Civilians, fearing slaughter by the Mexicans in the aftermath of the Alamo, joined the march east in what became known as the Runaway Scrape. Colonel Juan Seguín, a Tejano who had been a messenger for Travis, gathered a small troop to provide rearguard protection for the fleeing citizens.

Both Houston's troops and civilians grumbled that it was cowardly to flee rather than fight, but Houston had a plan. While the Mexican Army marched all over southeast Texas seeking engagement with the Texians, Houston held his troops on the Groce plantation on the east side of the Brazos River, near present-day Waller and southeast of Hempstead, and trained them for the fight to come.

The Battle of Goliad and the subsequent execution of an estimated four hundred men followed the fall of the Alamo. General James Fannin and his men, along with other insurgents, were captured after the Battle of Coleto (Goliad County). Still armed, they demanded treatment as prisoners of war, which according to the customs of civilized nations meant parole and a return to Texas. Santa Anna had obtained a decree from his government that all prisoners taken in arms against the government be treated as pirates and executed.

General José de Urrea had no stomach for executions; he convinced Fannin that his men should surrender their arms. But when Santa Anna demanded his executive order be carried out, Urrea left Goliad and turned the distasteful responsibility over to General José Nicholás de la Portilla. All of the prisoners, even the wounded, were shot, most by firing squads, or bayoneted. A few escaped into the woods, avoiding the firing squads, and some twenty men—physicians, interpreters, and others with essential skills—were saved by a woman known only to be a great beauty and now called the Angel of Goliad.

Up to that time, Santa Anna had been regarded as a cunning enemy. The massacre at Goliad, however, led Texians and the United States to brand Santa Anna and all Mexicans as cruel, a reputation that caused racial strife for generations. More immediately, the massacre aroused fury not only in North America but across the ocean in Great Britain and France. The outrage did much to promote the cause of Texas, but the cost in human life was high.

On April 18, 1836, Houston marched his troops east toward Harrisburg, in present-day Harris County, and established a camp in a protected wooded area on Buffalo Bayou. Houston received word that Santa Anna had set up camp nearby on an exposed plain near the San Jacinto River, a location an expert military commander would never have chosen. Houston ordered the bridge over Sims Bayou destroyed, thereby cutting off the only escape route open to either army. On the afternoon of April 21, Houston's men attacked. Their battle cry? "Remember the Alamo! Remember Goliad!"

Santa Anna was captured, and though he faced considerable criticism for his actions, Houston spared his enemy's life in order to end the fighting. Texas was at last independent from Mexico.

Over the years, the interpretations of the pivotal battle at the Alamo have changed. Immediately after, it seemed that the entire population of the United States saw it in the black-and-white terms of pure good against pure evil. In their eyes, the defending Texians were heroic martyrs to the cause of independence; the attacking Mexicans were devils in disguise, under the leadership of the greatest devil of them all, Santa Anna. Stories that came out of Texas would claim that a force of seven thousand Mexicans had attacked 189 men who were prepared to die for their ideals.

In truth, Santa Anna had about fifteen hundred men, most of them good and decent men who were fighting for their own country and defending their way of life. According to official accounts, 189 men died

Houston, Santa Anna, Cos. Library of Congress.

defending the Alamo; there may have been as many as 257 killed there that day. Not all of those who died were settlers filled with lofty ideals. Some were Tejanos—Mexicans who fought to oppose Santa Anna's dictatorship—and men who truly fought for independence and freedom. But some were also adventurers, renegades, men who would go anywhere for a good fight. We may never know the whole truth from the historical record. Santa Anna's official report, which surfaced years later, claimed a magnificent victory, inflating the number of Alamo defenders to about six hundred, praising the Mexican soldiers for their heroism in hand-to-hand combat. Santa Anna never acknowledged that the Texians managed to kill approximately six hundred Mexican soldiers before they succumbed to overwhelming numbers.

The fall of the Alamo is in some ways simply one of those stories that has taken on increasingly mythic proportions over the years. In part, it loomed large in American minds at the time because of the Texas and frontier heroes who died there alongside Colonel Travis—including

View of Alamo Plaza from the west, with the Medical Arts Building looming over the mission. Note the cars surrounding the site. Library of Congress, Historic American Building Survey, April 1938. Arthur W. Stewart, photographer.

Bowie, Crockett, and Bonham. Today, for many Texans, the Alamo story embodies all that we like to believe characterizes our larger-than-life state—fierce patriotism, courage, and the rebellion of the individual against authority. But this bit of history, as generally taught in schools and accepted by most as gospel, is a masculine story, full of bloodlust and courage—and all those qualities we associate with bold men.

The story was told over and over that this brave handful of Anglo men were defeated only by the overwhelming numbers of the Mexican Army under the brilliant general, Santa Anna. Other myths grew up about the battle, such as the story of Travis drawing a line in the sand. Some historians believe that never happened but was a product of the romanization of the battle. History has several similar stories of leaders drawing lines in the sand. It was generally believed that there were no survivors, but of course several women and children walked out of the chapel after the battle. And there are rumors to this day of a few Mexicans who survived by claiming to be prisoners of war.

That massacre, along with other Mexican victories during that campaign, also laid the groundwork for continuing racial conflict in Texas, particularly South Texas. Under Santa Anna, Mexicans earned a reputation for extreme cruelty. Survivors of the campaign and supporters of Texas independence claimed that the Mexican troops were bloodthirsty, without humanity. That, too, was an exaggeration. General Urrea stands as an example of a military leader with compassion, and there were other instances where an officer had either to follow Santa Anna's cruel orders or sacrifice his own life. Even today, charges of cruelty are sometimes leveled at the Mexican population. And, as noted, most of the Mexican soldiers were fighting less for bloodlust than to defend their homeland and preserve their way of life.

Racism goes both ways. In 2012, the mother of San Antonio then-mayor Julián Castro, Maria del Rosario Castro, a member of La Raza Unida, a group that fought for civil rights of Mexican Americans, told the *New York Times* that she grew up being told the Battle of the Alamo was "glorious," only to learn the so-called heroes were really "a bunch of drunks and crooks and slaveholding imperialists who conquered land that didn't belong to them." Her words incited an attack on her by Fox News, as reported by Paul Burka in *Texas Monthly*.

But don't say any of that to a true Texan. The story of the Alamo lives on as one of the great tales of the American West and of American grit and independence.

In truth, the story of the Alamo does not end with that 1836 battle and defeat. Nor is it always a men's story. The second Battle of the Alamo would be a women's battle, fought with the same determination shown by the original defenders but with different weapons—with words and money and sometimes with outrageous behavior. The battle became a personal one, waged by Adina De Zavala, a pioneer in historic preservation, and Clara Driscoll, Texas ranch heiress and philanthropist, in a time when women were rarely philanthropists. A different outcome to this second battle might not have changed the history of Texas much, but it would have robbed Texas and the United States of an icon, a symbol of the rich history of Texas. And it's time to share the story of the second battle

CHAPTER ONE

———◦•◦———

An Unlikely Alliance

A tiny woman, her skirt flying and her hair blowing without a hat to contain it, ran through the dusty streets of San Antonio, ignoring the horse-and-buggy taxis waiting to pick up passengers. She passed the bandstand in Alamo Plaza, barely glancing at the historic chapel or the long barracks. Rushing past the Crockett Block and the Maverick Building, she made her way to the Menger Hotel, a great square building, its covered portico guarded by a doorman. The building proudly flew the flag of the United States atop the three-story structure; the corners of the roof sported small cannons. Adina De Zavala always hoped they did not stand for the canons Santa Anna's army leveled against the Alamo defenders. Although she resented the commercial buildings that increasingly crowded and overshadowed the Spanish mission, she had come to accept the Menger Hotel, which had been on the Alamo Plaza almost all her life, having been built in 1859.

"Quick, tell me where I can find the hotel owners, the Kampmanns!" Adina was out of breath from her sprint, but she craned her neck to look up at the face of the tall bellman who stood stiff and straight at the door of the fine hotel, his brass buttons polished and gleaming.

Looking down, the bellman stared in puzzlement at this woman who had practically accosted him. She was clearly no longer young, probably nearing forty, he guessed. At the Menger, the finest hotel in San Antonio,

1

President Theodore Roosevelt speaking in front of the Alamo, 1905. The Hugo and Schmeltzer building is clearly evident. Library of Congress.

he was used to seeing women of high fashion. Narrow waists, softly flowing gowns, and large hats, often decorated with feathers, were de rigueur for the hotel's usual female guests. This breathless, frantic lady was no woman of society—she wore a plain shirtwaist tucked into a straight, bombazine skirt. Her head was bare and her hair—once probably neatly pinned atop her head—was windblown. She was clearly impatient with the fine manners usually expected of women.

When he shook his head as if to reject her request, she grabbed his arm and said forcefully, "Tell me! I must see them immediately!"

Disentangling her hand from his arm and lightly brushing off his jacket, he said softly and courteously, "Ma'am, I cannot rightly tell you where you can find them," with as much dignity as he could muster. "The Kampmanns left yesterday for their annual French vacation."

"No, that can't be right," Adina said, as she sank to the curb, her face buried in her hands, her skirt crumpled beneath her, her shirtwaist now loose and wrinkled from her run.

"Tell me what's the matter," the bellman drawled in his low, Southern accent, his attitude toward this obviously distraught woman softening, "perhaps I can help."

She threw her hands up in exasperation. "No one can help now. It's too late. All my hard work is over. I might as well jump in the San Antonio River. They were my last hope!"

Her despair was clearly difficult for the bellman to ignore. "Now, it can't be as bad as all that," he replied. "What business did you have with the Kampmanns?"

"Well, I didn't really have any business with them, at least, not yet, but I hoped to," Adina said. "I'm in a dilemma. I need to buy the San Antonio de Valero Mission."

The confused bellman stared across the plaza at the crumbling mission and then asked, "Why would you want that crumbling old chapel?"

Little attention, either governmental or popular, had been paid to the buildings of the Alamo mission during the nineteenth century, but the glory of the defenders had grown steadily over the seventy years since the famous siege and massacre. The doomed Texians killed that day in March 1836, were seen as the heroes in the battle for Texas independence. And there was a widespread misconception in San Antonio and elsewhere, one that lingers today, that the chapel at the Alamo mission was where the defenders died, rather than the long barracks, where the final battle actually took place.

Toward the end of the nineteenth century, the Alamo Monumental Society—formed by a group of interested preservationists— campaigned for the state to buy the chapel from the Catholic Church, which had owned the buildings of the old mission since 1841. In 1883, the church deeded the chapel building to the State of Texas; the state, in turn, deeded it to the City of San Antonio. Hoping to attract tourists, the city used pictures of the Alamo extensively in advertisements but cut out the surrounding city scenes. Visitors to the actual site were

The Alamo Fort and Menger Hotel, showing what remained of the long barracks before reconstruction. Prints and Photographs Collection, The Dolph Briscoe Center for American History, The University of Texas at Austin.

often disappointed, calling it an embarrassment to the city. The city also apparently made no effort to renovate the decaying chapel building after taking ownership, despite its supposed historic significance. Alamo historian Richard Winders, PhD, has suggested that San Antonio was busy trying to become a progressive, modern city, shedding its reputation as a Mexican town. So bond money went for modern civic improvements, while the Alamo decayed.

Part of the reason for visitors' disappointment in the Alamo buildings may have been what had happened to the actual site of the defenders' last stand. The long barracks, the old convent building that was adjacent to the chapel, had actually been privately owned since 1877, when a merchant named Honoré Grenet purchased the building from the church. Grenet covered the two-story stone walls of the long barracks with a wooden superstructure and used the building for a museum and grocery store. Grenet would claim that he built the wooden superstructure to approximate the appearance of the building at the time of the massacre and to keep the history of the brave martyrs alive in the minds of the people of San Antonio and Texas. Any resemblance was difficult to discern. The wooden superstructure became a bulletin board on which various poster and flyers were displayed, an eyesore next to the charming chapel façade. Most people didn't know that the Alamo chapel's distinctive look had been constructed by the U.S. Army when they used the building for a storage depot.

After Grenet's death, the long barracks structure, complete with its stock and the "good will of the business" was purchased by the grocery firm of Hugo and Schmeltzer. Presumably the company wished to capitalize on the grocery trade already established by Grenet. Hugo and Schmeltzer apparently considered the building of commercial value only and gave casual recognition to its historical significance. The firm removed some of Grenet's additions but left the superstructure and, some thought, created an eyesore of their own.

When the grocery firm moved their business elsewhere in San Antonio, they used the long barracks for storage. The deterioration continued, and the city finally condemned the structure, declaring it unsafe. Hugo and Schmeltzer decided to put the building on the market.

In the early 1890s in San Antonio, a woman named Adina De Zavala had organized a group of like-minded women interested in Texas history. She called them the De Zavala Daughters and stated their goal as the preservation of Texas historical sites. In addition to preserving missions and other sites of historic significance, De Zavala Daughters would ensure that schools were named after prominent Texans (schools were previously designated by numbers), as Adina maintained that naming schools after heroes would give children a more meaningful learning experience. The De Zavala Daughters also worked to see that important dates in Texas history were suitably recognized and celebrated as official holidays—March 2 for the declaration of independence from Mexico; March 6 for the fall of the Alamo; and April 21 as San Jacinto Day.

In 1893, the organization became a chapter of the larger Daughters of the Republic of Texas, commonly known as the DRT. The DRT had been formed in Galveston by Betty and Hally Ballinger and chartered by the State of Texas in 1895 to preserve the memory of those who died during the Texas Revolution and to further historical research. The goals of the group, which had first called itself Daughters of the Lone Star Republic, closely aligned to those of the De Zavala group. The alliance with the DRT strengthened Adina's resolve to preserve the Alamo's long barracks.

As early as 1892, Adina De Zavala had approached Gustav Schmeltzer about the possibility of the De Zavala Daughters purchasing the long barracks of the Alamo Mission for preservation. Unlike most San Antonians, Adina knew that the long barracks—not the chapel—had been the site of the defenders' last resistance against Santa Anna's troops. Mr. Schmeltzer recorded his various transactions with Adina in a 1908 memo, recalling of their first meeting that he fully approved of her project to utilize the building as a Hall of Fame and Museum of History. With Mr. Hugo and the other owners, Schmeltzer agreed that they would offer the De Zavala Daughters the first right to purchase the property when they were ready to sell, and that the price to the chapter would be $75,000—the owners would discount the strict commercial value of the structure by $10,000.

For whatever reason, the campaign to make the purchase was slow in starting, but in 1900, Adina announced the De Zavala Daughters were ready to begin fund-raising for the purchase, and she would be traveling to Houston and Galveston for that purpose. In Galveston, she barely missed the deadly hurricane that devastated the island city and killed an estimated ten thousand people, and perhaps as a result of that tragedy, formal large-scale fund-raising for the cause was postponed until 1903. By then, however, Adina was a familiar figure on the streets of San Antonio as she gathered donations to save the Alamo.

Despite Schmeltzer's promise to her, when the time came for the grocery firm to finally divest the property, Adina was not the first to hear of

Adina De Zavala, probably about the time of the second battle. Adina Emilia De Zavala Papers, The Dolph Briscoe Center for American History, The University of Texas at Austin.

the pending sale of the barracks. In 1903, Pompeo Coppini, an Italian sculptor who had immigrated to San Antonio and was hoping for artistic commissions, learned of the sale when he was talking with architect Harvey Page about one of his works. Page mentioned that a commission was pending for a ten-foot heroic marble statue of Davy Crockett that was to be installed in a hotel to be built on the present site of the disgraceful long barracks.

Coppini and Adina had become good friends since his arrival in the city. He had sought her out to help him pursue his interest in learning Texas history so that he could be better informed about his new home and possible commissions. He had also supported her attempts to open a School of Art in San Antonio, an effort that was ultimately thwarted by the school board. Because Coppini had learned his Alamo history from Adina, he turned down the possible commission. He knew the barracks were sacred ground. Harvey Page argued that no one in San Antonio cared enough about preserving the old building to contribute a nickel to saving it, but Coppini knew better. Adina De Zavala cared.

When Coppini left the architect's office, he rushed to Adina's lodgings. Rubbing his hands together with agitation, he burst out, "Miss Adina, you and my wife, you go out every day to beg lumber and other materials from merchants, so you can repair fences around missions, like the Alamo."

"Yes," Adina said, puzzled but still calm.

"Sit down," she went on, trying to soothe him. "May I get you some coffee?"

"No, no. You must hear this. If you do not find a way to buy the Hugo-Schmeltzer building now, the long barracks will be torn down and another hotel built. I was just offered a commission to put a heroic-size statue of Davy Crockett in the lobby." He gestured with his hands, indicating the larger-than-life size of the proposed art work.

"No, no. I cannot do it," Coppini expressed his alarm. "You have taught me. That is sacred ground. We cannot have a hotel there."

As soon as he left, Adina raced to the Menger Hotel to explore the only hope she had for saving the historic structure.[1] And the bellman had just demonstrated the battle that she faced.

She favored the young man with a withering look, as if she were tired of people who didn't understand about the Alamo. Then, patiently, she explained, as she must have many times before, "Not the chapel. The long barracks, where Hugo and Schmeltzer has their grocery now—that's where the Alamo defenders fought and died. After the grocery company bought the long barracks, in 1892, they gave me a verbal promise that if they were ever going to sell the building, the De Zavala Daughters would have the first chance at buying the property." As an afterthought, she added, "I organized that chapter of the Daughters of the Republic in 1892 for just such an emergency."

Adina went on, "If they don't sell it to me, developers will tear it down and put up a hotel in its place. I talked to the people at Hugo-Schmeltzer and managed to cut a deal. They said if I could come up with the money, why, they'd sell *me* the property, instead!"

The bellman, still bewildered, protested, "It's just a jumble of tumbled-down decaying bricks with a few old bullet holes here and there. Whatever made you think that a group of women could raise enough money to buy that building? It could be used for a lot of things."

"Tumble-downed bricks? Bullet holes?" she cried, jumping up and punching him on the arm. "Have you no sense of history? Have you no honor? Have you no respect for your ancestors?"

The bellman looked at her in amazement and took a step back. Trying not to lose his temper at this hot-headed lady, he said, "Well, ma'am, truth be told, I've only been here a month, I'm from Tennessee and haven't yet learned a lot about the area."

"That *relic*, young man," she said with all the fire she could muster, "just happens to be the site of one of the most significant battles of the Texas Revolution, the place where two hundred early Texians stood their ground against the entire Mexican Army. Every male soldier died in that siege. Only a few women and children were spared to tell the tale!"

"Well, I don't know anything about that," he said sheepishly, "but tell me why you were so all-bent on seeing the Kampmanns?"

"If you knew your Texas history, which you obviously don't, you would know that they're descended from some of the first Texans and are extremely patriotic and would do anything for this grand state. I was going to see if they would put up the money to buy the Alamo to keep it from being torn down." She was so angry that tears began to roll down her cheeks. "Now, who knows what will happen to it?"

The bellman brightened. "You know," he said, "there's someone here who might be able to help you. I may not know much about Texas history, but we have a lady up on the second floor, and I hear her father owns just about all of South Texas. And I understand that South Texas is where most of the oil is. You know, that place called Spindletop and all around it."

"A lady?" Adina wasted only a moment looking ruefully at her rumpled clothes.

The bellman went on. "I reckon she's got a nice little pile of money herself, if her daddy's that rich. At least my boss told me to take real good care of her because she's got enough money to buy our hotel and fire us all if we don't treat her right."

"Really?" Adina asked, intrigued. "What's her name?"

"Miss Clara Driscoll. And she seems to be about twenty-something, if she's a day. She's in Room 217. And if you say I told you so, I'll lose my job. But I hate to see a lady cry," he said, handing her his handkerchief.

"Clara Driscoll? The one that's been writing about the Alamo in the newspaper? Room 217. Clara Driscoll. *Gracias, amigo!*" she said as she

The young heiress Clara Driscoll, circa 1905. DRT Collection at Texas A&M University-San Antonio.

raced toward the grand staircase, lifting her skirt as she flew up the stairs, two at a time, in her haste to reach Clara's room. Composing herself, she stopped for a moment to let her breath return to normal before knocking. She could barely keep herself from pounding on the heavy wooden door.

"Yes?" Clara said, answering the door. "Who are you?"

"My name is Adina De Zavala, Miss Driscoll. You don't know me, at least not yet, but I need your help. May I come in?"

From Mission to Fortification
to Sacred Shrine

When the mission system in Texas began to fade away, the mission at San Antonio de Bexar was secularized. Starting in 1793, it saw multiple uses. When the Alamo de Parra cavalry unit, so named because most of the men came from the village of Alamo in Mexico, occupied the site in 1806, they used the long barracks—the old convent—for a military hospital, with patients on the second floor and soldiers' quarters on the first. The unfinished chapel building was still roofless, and by the 1820s, it had largely collapsed upon itself, but the two-story 180-foot-long structure attached to the northwest corner of the chapel was solid. Near the mission stood a small grove of cottonwood trees, which underlined the suitability of the name. *Alamo* is the Spanish word for "cottonwood."

The first savior of the Alamo—of the buildings on the site—was said to be Anastacio Bustamante, military commandant of the Eastern Provinces who later went on to become president of Mexico. In 1827, legislation was proposed that would have put rock from the Texas missions on the block at public auction. Bustamante demanded the mission be preserved intact so it could be used by military troops.

In 1835, when General Santa Anna sent his brother-in-law, General Martín Perfecto de Cos, and a contingent of soldiers to stop the Texian insurgency, the troops occupied the Alamo, but the Texians soon routed them and retook the site. Cos signed a treaty, promising to take his unit back to Mexico and never return to Texas territory. This defeat infuriated Santa Anna, who immediately assembled a much larger army for a return to Texas. It is said that when General Sam Houston heard of Santa Anna's preparations for invasion, he ordered anything that could be used by the Mexican Army blown up. This would have, of course, included the Alamo.[2]

After the siege and massacre, the mission buildings sat empty from 1836 until 1849, and as unoccupied buildings will do, it continued to deteriorate. Looters carried off loose stones, and the chapel remained roofless. In 1841, the Republic of Texas gave the Catholic Church claim to the chapel and adjoining property as well as to other missions throughout the territory. After Texas achieved statehood, the church allowed the federal government to use the Alamo as an arsenal and warehouse. In 1849, the government repaired the chapel, giving it a peaked roof and its distinctive stair-step and loop parapet, which was designed to hide the efficient but undistinguished peak. That façade, of course, added more than thirteen years after the battle, gives the structure its iconic look to this day, featured in pictures and tourists' minds.

During the Civil War, the federal government surrendered the property to the Confederacy, though it still technically belonged to the church. In 1865, the Bishop of San Antonio decided to turn the mission over to the German Catholic community in the city and directed his secretary and vice chancellor to notify the federal government to vacate the property. The major general in charge of the depot replied that the government had repaired the building and made it suitable for grain storage at its own expense and that vacating would be inconvenient. The struggle over the buildings' custodianship and occupation lasted several years and became a moot point in the 1870s, when the federal government built an army depot. The army vacated the mission building in 1876. The long-term result, though, was that the Catholic Church lost the Alamo as a parish due to the drawn-out dispute. The German Catholics had found a home nearby, and when the Alamo chapel at last became available, it was too close to the German place of worship to justify establishing another parish.

By the time the army left, in 1871, the only portions of the original complex remaining were the chapel and the long barracks—or convent. The west wall and low barracks were completely gone, and only the foundation of the wall remained.

CHAPTER TWO

―――――•●•―――――

The Inimitable Adina

Adina De Zavala's interest in historic preservation was not new, nor was it surprising given her heritage. She was the granddaughter of Lorenzo de Zavala, a man who had signed the Texas Declaration of Independence, had helped draft the constitution of the Republic of Texas, and had been elected the first vice president of the Republic of Texas.[3] A native of Yucatán, de Zavala was descended from Spanish immigrants to Mexico and was described as well-educated and extremely bright. He had careers as a newspaper editor, political leader, physician, and author. Active in the first government of Mexico after it gained independence from Spain, he was devoted to the idea of representative democracy. Among other posts, he served as minister of finance, ambassador to France, and a provincial governor. De Zavala and Antonio López de Santa Anna were once colleagues, but when Santa Anna introduced his military dictatorship in Mexico, de Zavala spoke out loudly against his former colleague. He was imprisoned for a time in Mexico, during which he taught himself the skills of a physician.

Many in Mexico would label de Zavala a traitor when—after his release—he fled to Texas in 1835, establishing a home at Zavala Point on Buffalo Bayou. His background in politics, language skills, and administrative knowledge made him eminently suitable for becoming a part of the government of the new Republic of Texas. After he helped draft the constitution for the republic, and after Santa Anna's defeat at San Jacinto, he was part of a peacekeeping mission to Mexico. The mission failed, which de Zavala attributed to sabotage from the Texian side—he was convinced that the Texians wanted independence, not peace. Returning home, discouraged, de Zavala remained committed to a workable future for Texas and its southern neighbor and former mother country.

After the Battle of San Jacinto, de Zavala insisted that Mexican prisoners, including Santa Anna, be returned to Mexico, according to the terms of the treaty. Many Texans disagreed, and he was criticized, his loyalty to Texas questioned. In Mexico, he was scorned for his advocacy for Texans. De Zavala might almost be considered a man without a country.

De Zavala's first wife, Teresa Currea, had died after years of poor health shortly after the family moved to Texas. She and de Zavala had two children, Lorenzo Jr. and Manuela. He had met his second wife, Emily West, in New York. They were the parents of two daughters and a son, Augustine, who was the father of Adina De Zavala. Adina's mother, Julia Tyrrell de Zavala, was born in Ireland and was of, as Adina always specified, "patrician" background. Adina was born in 1861, so she never knew her illustrious grandfather, who had died in late 1836 after a boating accident.

A curious story about Lorenzo de Zavala's second wife, Emily West de Zavala, has caused some confusion about Adina De Zavala's parentage. Emily was evidently of mixed race—though whether that fact was obvious is debatable. However, in that era, any amount of black ancestry was enough to invoke laws of segregation and discrimination. For example, free blacks could then travel to Texas but were not allowed to settle within the state. When Emily West de Zavala traveled to Texas in 1835 aboard the passenger ship *The Flash*, a second Emily West was also listed as a passenger on board, this one a professed woman of color the same age of Emily de Zavala. The second Emily was purportedly traveling to Texas to protect the property of one James Morgan. Some historians find this concurrence of names and race too great a coincidence and suspect that Emily double-booked herself as a free black and a white woman on the trip in order to forestall trouble. She would be able to claim whichever identity gave her easy passage into the state.

The fascinating biography of a woman named Emily West is further complicated by the tale that Santa Anna himself had snatched her from the boat and held her captive. It has long been accepted by historians that Santa Anna had a woman named Emily in his tent at San Jacinto when the Texans launched their attack at the hour of siesta. Some even suggest that she was a spy for Houston. But it seems unlikely that this Emily was actually Emily West de Zavala, by that time a married woman with three children. Some historians call the whole story a "fine temptation" with no proof, particularly the part that has Santa Anna snatching Emily from the boat. Still, there is also the rumor, floated even today, that Lorenzo de Zavala had a longstanding affair with the woman known as the Yellow Rose of Texas, the purported spy who helped bring down Santa Anna. It was a tale that some say would have embarrassed granddaughter Adina, but it was also likely a story that would have piqued her interest in learning more about history. Most likely, there were two women named Emily involved in this story; de Zavala married one of them, and the other was the famed Yellow Rose of Texas.[4] But the tangled story is indeed a fine temptation to ponder.

The oldest of Augustine and Julia de Zavala's six surviving children, Adina was homeschooled first by her mother and grandmother and then by family governesses. Education was very important to the de Zavalas, and Adina was proud of her own intellect and schooling. She once told an interviewer that she could not remember a time when she could not read. And when the family moved from their home at Buffalo Bayou—which probably was part of an *empresario* land grant to Lorenzo de

Zavala—to Galveston in 1871, Adina and her sister enrolled in the Ursu-
line Academy there. Adina apparently carried memories of the home at
Buffalo Bayou the rest of her life. In an 1934 interview for the *Dallas
Morning News*, she recalled the roses that bloomed in the garden.

During the Civil War, Adina's father, Augustine de Zavala was a
blockade runner, and afterward he still made his living on the water. But
the moist climate of Galveston was hard on his health. Adina could not
recall a time when he did not suffer with rheumatism. Probably around
1873, the family moved again, this time to the San Antonio area, purchasing land on what became known as De Zavala Road.

Late in her life, Adina would reminisce about her childhood and
speculate that her love of Texas history was sparked by the stories of her
grandfather that she heard from her parents, her surviving grandparents,
and Augustine's friends who often came to visit the family. Augustine, by
then a farmer, also sometimes hitched up his horse and buggy to go visiting with old friends, many of them veterans, and he often took Adina on
these jaunts to hear the stories of the war for independence, the Alamo,
Goliad, and San Jacinto. From Adina's earliest days, she felt her family
background gave her a special connection to Texas history.

"I loved history," she once recalled. "My sister and I used to put on
historical plays of our own creation."

Adina frequently explained her belief that children are impressed
by objects and pageantry—a belief that accounted for the importance
she placed on the visible symbols of Texas history such as the Alamo.
She said that if a child can see the room where a historical figure lived,
or an object touched by that figure, history becomes more alive and
meaningful. She called her teaching method "digging out" history, and
her own home was filled with what she would have called "object lessons"—carved chairs, cabinets, and tables, all heirlooms from France
and Spain. An interviewer visiting her at home once examined an old
plowshare on display, leading Adina to exclaim, "It was hand welded in

Adina and her dog, in doorway. DRT Collection at Texas A&M University-San Antonio.

Old Spain, probably the middle of the seventeenth century." Apparently, the plowshare had been brought to the New World by the padres who established the missions, and to Adina it was tangible evidence of a story worth keeping.

No doubt a favorite story—despite its tragic end—was that of Lorenzo de Zavala's boating accident on Buffalo Bayou. He had taken four-year-old Augustine boating, and when the boat overturned, de Zavala was able to get Augustine back into the boat once he righted it. Lorenzo swam to shore, pushing the boat ahead of him, his son safe. It was November, and the water and weather were both cold. It was in the aftermath of this episode that de Zavala died from exposure.

Another story that thrilled Adina was told by her uncle, Lorenzo de Zavala Jr. At the age of twenty-one, when the young Lorenzo was fighting with Houston's army at San Jacinto, he was called to be a translator for Houston and Santa Anna. Lorenzo Jr. would share the details of this event in three letters to Adina, the first written when she was still in school and the last in 1895, fifty-nine years after the battle, recalling the scene under the oak tree where Houston rested an injured ankle.[5] Adina's roots in the revolution were deep.

At the age of seventeen, after her time at the Ursuline Academy, Adina enrolled in the opening year of what was then called Sam Houston Normal Institute, in Huntsville, Texas.[6] After earning her teaching degree at the institute, she next attended a school of music in Chillicothe, Missouri. Despite the expectations of the era and the relative wealth and prestige of the de Zavala family, Adina was set on a career, not marriage—and specifically a career in education. She taught first in Terrell, Texas, and then in Austin. In 1886, when she was twenty-five, she returned to San Antonio, where she taught in various elementary schools for the next twenty years.

As a teacher, Adina was never intimidated by rules or conventions. Once she protested her salary and grade classification in person at a school board meeting in San Antonio. Her protest led the board to ban personal appeals, accepting complaints only by letter. She lived by her own rules, once failing to appear in her classroom until the second month of the school year. Her explanation was that she had been studying Mexican history in Mexico. Frustrated by bureaucracy, she attended teachers' meetings only when she "had nothing better to attend to."

Adina would never marry, although there is some evidence that she had an attachment to a man in Fort Worth when she was about thirty. The gentleman in question, however, eventually married someone else. Over the years, one or two men who expressed an interest in wooing Adina were gently rebuffed. Her study of history and her pursuit of professional success and satisfaction let Adina to escape the obligations of marriage and running a household. But there may have been more to the story. One scholar suggests that Adina's difficulty in forming lasting relationships stemmed from a testy relationship with her mother, Julia. Adina's choice of a single life may have been inspired, at least in part, by the negative example of marriage she saw in her parents' union. Apparently, Julia de Zavala was a rigid and unhappy woman, and the relationship between Adina's parents was not one of wedded bliss. Eventually, Julia also became estranged from one of her sons.

Adina was never domestically inclined. Her work and papers created chaos wherever she was, and though she could cook, she rarely did more than prepare subsistence meals. Living with her mother and sisters was difficult enough; a husband and children would have taken energy she preferred to spend on her work.

Adina's seemingly endless energy for work and organization and enthusiasm for Texas history had led her to establish the De Zavala Daughters and then to join the DRT specifically with preservation of historic landmarks in mind. In her opinion, the very best way to honor the past was to preserve its structures—a continuation of her "digging out" philosophy. By the time the sale of the long-barracks building was planned by Hugo and Schmeltzer, saving that long-abused and ruined building had become the focus of Adina's dedication to the preservation of the story of Texas. However, because of her leadership of the De Zavala chapter, Adina knew that neither the De Zavala Daughters nor the larger DRT had anything close to the funds necessary to act on the option to buy the Hugo and Schmeltzer property when the possibility of a sale became more of a certainty with the interest of the hotel syndicate. Still, when the hotel developers seemed set on a path to buy the mission and demolish it, she didn't allow the lack of funds to stop her for more than a moment. The developers thought only of adding to San Antonio's commercial success with its hotel. Adina thought only of the men who had died on that fateful day in 1836.

Adina needed $75,000 fast—and from a private source. Business leaders in San Antonio would never support her cause. They were encouraged by the economic benefits that had already come from the commercial properties going up around the Alamo Plaza, crowding it and distracting tourists from the historic spot itself.

And that's how Adina De Zavala ended up banging on the door of Miss Clara Driscoll's suite at the Menger.

Starting at the end of the fifteenth century, the race was on among the superpowers of Europe to gain a foothold in the newly discovered North American continent. Spain was one of the earliest to send out explorers and establish colonies in the New World, and part of the plan to establish and maintain commanding presence was introducing the mission system. Ostensibly intended to create an institutional system to convert the native population to Christianity, establishing and manning missions across the territory also promoted the adoption of Spanish culture and solidified its control over the region. At the system's height, Texas was home to between twenty-five and thirty-five missions.

While some records indicate that there was a mission in what is now Texas as early as the fifteenth century, the missions really flourished in the seventeenth and eighteenth centuries, before virtually disappearing in the early 1800s prior to the Texas War for Independence. Three schools of friars of the Catholic Church established these missions—Dominicans, Franciscans, and Jesuits, but it was the state that had the real control.

The Spanish government enjoyed *patronato real* (royal patronage) and controlled the missions tightly. The government decided where a mission would be located, who could be missionaries, how many friars would be at any given site, and set all general policies for each mission in the system. Spanish officials had learned the hard way that leaving control of the native population to soldiers and civilians had often resulted in abuses and in the enslavement of the indigenous people. Putting the church, ostensibly, in charge was intended to change that.

Friars coming north from Mexico City brought with them cattle, other livestock, vegetables, plows and other farm tools, horses and their harnesses, bridles, and saddles, and the Spanish language. Along with the Catholic religion, the native population learned such skills as blacksmithing to care for the livestock and carpentry and masonry to build the missions. Women were taught to weave and provide clothing for the friars and the general population.

When natives accepted Catholicism, they often lived in the missions, most of which were surrounded by a protective wall. The mission also owned unprotected farms and ranches outside the wall. Spain planned to establish a presidio, or military fort, near each mission, but it didn't always work out. The Presidio of San Antonio de Béxar, which would have protected the Alamo, was never completed. While the natives who accepted the Spanish presence were generally peace-loving hunters and gatherers, the missions were in constant danger from the warlike Apaches until the mid-eighteenth century and then from the Comanche, who swept down from the north and began raiding in Texas after the Apache lost control. Frequently, the native population who had accepted Christianity and moved into the missions provided their own defense from behind the mission wall.

The goal of the mission program was "secularization." Spaniards expected the Indians to "grow into" Christianity, at which time the efforts to convert would not be necessary, and the natives would live in civil societies, albeit societies that mirrored Spanish culture. Some of Texas's major cities grew out of missions that were successfully secularized. Unfortunately, secularization carried with it the racial and class distinctions of Spanish society in general.

The downside of converting and "civilizing" the peaceful tribes was that those peoples were usually semi-nomadic and not used to staying permanently in one place. They would spend months in a mission, but the seasons for hunting and gathering called them to wander.

The friars also unwittingly brought European diseases, such as smallpox, to the native population. Eventually native populations dwindled, due to periodic epidemics and the slow growth rate of the population. The decrease in population of the areas around the missions, as well as floods, crop failures, and aggressive acts by Spanish soldiers, all contributed to the eventual collapse of the mission system. What were previously communal properties were then privatized, often falling into the hands of ranchers and businessmen who simply wanted the property.

The influence of the missions is evident in Texas today in place names—such towns as Cuero, Lamesa, Laredo, Mexia (do *not* pronounce the "x"—it is a soft "j" sound), Plano. Words from Spanish commonly used in Texas include *hombre* (man), *arroyo* (a gully with steep sides and, when flooding, fast water), *que?* (what?), *mas* (more), *casa* and *casita* (house and little house), *padre* (father, secular or religious), *carne* (meat), *agua* (water). In architecture, the Spanish Colonial style lives on in low-pitched tile roofs, arched doorways and windows, courtyards, and the use of stucco and adobe.

CHAPTER THREE

———•••———

An Unlikely Savior

W hen twenty-three-year-old Clara Driscoll responded to the pounding on the door of her suite at the Menger Hotel, she had never met Adina De Zavala before. Nor would she ever have had reason to encounter the forty-two-year old teacher and historian. Although both were members of the DRT, they came from totally different worlds.

Like Adina, Clara was a native Texian, born in the no longer surviving town of St. Mary's on the South Texas coast. Both sets of her grandparents had helped settle land grants in Refugio and Goliad Counties in the years before the Texas Revolution. Clara could claim Irish blood, much like Adina. Her paternal grandfather, Daniel O'Driscoll, an immigrant, had arrived in this country in time to fight Santa Anna at the Battle of San Jacinto and had received one of the two hundred land grants made available to veterans of that campaign before the Republic of Texas declared that all public lands belonged to the state. Later in life, O'Driscoll owned a tavern in the town of Refugio, located about twenty miles from Corpus Christi; his grandson, Robert, would later buy ranches adjoining the original land grant. A history of the Driscoll family can be found at http://www.larosa-ranch.com.

On her mother's side, Clara was also connected to the Battle of San Jacinto. Her mother's parents had emigrated from England and settled in Texas in time for the grandfather, James Fox, to fight at the battle. James's daughter, who would become Clara's mother, was a teacher, and Julia's brother was for many years the foreman for the Driscoll ranches in South Texas. It was there that Julia would meet Robert Driscoll.

Clara's father, Robert, and his brother, Jeremiah, were raised near Refugio and fought in Virginia during the Civil War. Both returned home safely at the war's end, bringing with them nothing but their tattered uniforms and exhausted horses. They pooled their dreams and energies working cattle for a variety of ranchers and were paid in land from neighboring counties. As their ranch holdings grew, the brothers began to raise their own cattle and, over the years, became wealthy landowners, cattle ranchers, and businessmen, operating mostly in the Corpus Christi area. By the time Clara was born, in 1881, her father and uncle were millionaires.

Robert Driscoll was described as a man of medium height with brown eyes and hair. He picked up the nickname "Colonel" because of his proud, upright, military bearing. Even when he was young, some of the ranch hands referred to him as "the old man," out of respect. He loved to tell stories of his early, difficult years working the range, demonstrating his grit and establishing his credibility as a self-made man. He was clearly a tough man—a survivor and a hard worker.

On cattle drives, Driscoll took part in the work alongside his ranch hands and wore chaps, boots, and bandana, but on business trips to Corpus Christi and other population centers, he dressed conservatively as a businessman. Those who didn't know better would never have taken him for a rancher. Working together with other owners of large South Texas spreads, such as Robert J. Kleberg and John G. Kenedy, Driscoll helped bring the railroad to the Gulf Coast. To attract settlers who would support the railroad, he offered town sites and agricultural land from his own vast holdings as incentives.

Driscoll's business interests led to him becoming one of the first bankers in South Texas. He made cash loans to farmers and ranchers, and when it was time for the loans to be repaid, he told his debtors they could pay him in money or land, but that he preferred to be paid in land. Robert Driscoll accumulated land. A lot of land.

A renowned marksman, Driscoll used to take his son and daughter hunting with him on the ranch. If Driscoll had a weak spot, it was his deep love for his only daughter, Clara, who was several years younger than her brother and was indulged from birth. A favorite outing for the trio was coyote chasing on the ranch.

When she was still a young girl, her father, Robert, purchased the Palo Alto Ranch, eighteen miles outside the city of Corpus Christi, Texas. Clara's formative years were spent on the family ranch. Describing her childhood home, Clara once said, "If you stand on our porch nothing obstructs the vision for twenty miles. Back of our house is a raw field of oak trees that line the banks of a river. 'Palo Alto' is Mexican for high timber, from which we named our ranch. Moss hangs in festoons from the branches and fairly dips in the waters of the river. 'Agua Dulci' (Spanish for sweet water) we call the river. Sweet name, isn't it?"

The land, which she would later capture in words when she began writing fiction, was arid brushland, hostile to men and cattle alike. Clearing brush, which was done laboriously by hand, was a never-ending chore—it grew back as fast as a man could clear it. Drought was a chronic problem, and irrigation was essential to growing crops and raising livestock. Gradually the Driscolls were able to tame the land, replacing brush with grain crops and usable grasses. They eventually owed their fortune to cattle, cotton, and oil and gas wells.

Most of the surrounding area was inhabited by people from Mexico, and Clara's father hired Mexican cowboys and bronco busters to work the cattle. An article in the *World Magazine*, published in 1905, speculates that since most of the household help at Palo Alto were also from Mexico, Clara learned Spanish right along with English. She also learned much about Mexican culture, as well as folk music and dance. However, Robert Driscoll almost always employed Americans to supervise the Mexican workers, and Clara probably absorbed some of this subtle racial distinction at an early age.

Because of the relative isolation of the Driscoll ranch in the Palo Alto country, Clara had no close neighbors or playmates her own age as a child. Instead, until she was about eleven and her mother took her to New York, Clara's playmates were the Mexican cowboys who taught her to ride almost as soon as she could get up on a horse. She rode the most spirited of her father's horses and learned to handle both a rifle and a revolver. She wasn't afraid to try anything the cowboys would do. "There is only one thing I never learned to do," she would later say, "and that was to use the lariat. The others could do that for me, and some of the men at times 'roped' some pretty strange pets." Clara recalled her childhood pets for the *World Magazine* article.

Those strange pets included a wildcat cub that Clara named Perdito and assorted javelinas. An early photograph shows Clara holding her pet wildcat. "One of the boys brought in the wildcat when he was only a few months old," she said. "I named him Perdito, or Little Waif. When the picture was made, he was three years old. He was always very, very gentle with me. The funniest of my pets were javelinas, a species of wild hog which we have in our country. Lean, razor-backed fellows with long tusks. It is as dangerous to hunt them as the wild boars of Europe. In fact, they are the most vicious of our animals in the Southwest. I had two of these fellows for a long time."

In fact, the family's prairie land offered a flourishing habitat for all kinds of wild animals, including a large population of rattlesnakes. Clara was not allowed to ride out onto the dangerous prairie without a cowboy or *vaquero* in attendance. And when she did ride out or go on a hunt, she wore a khaki divided skirt, leggings, a broad-brimmed sombrero,

Clara in a riding habit around the turn of the century. Driscoll Foundation Endowment Fund of the Driscoll Children's Hospital in Corpus Christi, Texas.

and a tightly fitting corduroy jacket—clothing designed for comfort and protection.

Typically, when she sighted a coyote on one of her rides, she would signal the cowboy who rode with her who would lead her horse away after she dismounted. On one fateful occasion, she approached a cluster of coyotes feasting on a carcass, which made her indignant. The pack had killed one of her father's calves. Sensing danger, the coyotes melted away from the carcass, but they would be back. Clara hid in the brush until the coyotes started to return to their feast. Then, with her .44-caliber Colt carbine, she picked off the first hungry animal that returned to its prey. In the interview for *World Magazine*, Clara said of the incident: "It's a right queer sensation to be left alone surrounded by these beasts, but I wanted a big coyote rug, and I think I have skins enough now."

Clara's accounts of her feats and escapades on the ranch were always larger than life. Another story had her serving briefly as a deputy sheriff, enlisted to help protect her father's property against thieves. Rustlers and "fence cutters" had begun raiding Driscoll land and stealing cattle. On one of their raids, they shot and killed the elderly foreman of the ranch, a man who had been good to Clara and who she treasured. She was determined that proper justice would be done, no matter the circumstances. The problem was that the sheriff or the Texas Ranger were usually miles away when they were most needed. According to Clara's account of the events that ensued, she wanted to catch the rustlers before they left her father's land, but she would not allow the cowboys to lynch them—a common enough occurrence in a place where law enforcement was scarce. Clara insisted that she wanted no lynch law on her ranch. According to Richard Ables article, trouble with rustlers at the Driscoll ranch was first reported in the *St. Louis Post-Dispatch*.

Clara would later state that she went to Sheriff J. C. Tobin of Mexico County with a proposal:

"If you make me a deputy, I'd be an officer of the law, and I could help you catch those thieves. I'm as good with a rifle as any man on the ranch, except maybe my father. You can ask him."

The sheriff likely stared at the slight teenage girl standing in front of him, fists set belligerently on her hips. He wouldn't have had to ask her father about her ability with a rifle. Clara's marksmanship was already legendary in her part of Texas, but he warned her against her bravado.

"You know those men won't care if you're a grown man or a girl. Given the chance, they'll kill you." His voice dropped dramatically. "Or worse."

"They won't get a chance," she said confidently.

Perhaps recognizing that Clara Driscoll was a law unto herself, he apparently said, "I never thought I'd be swearing in a young girl. Place your left hand on the Bible and raise your right hand." He repeated the age-old question, asking if she solemnly swore to uphold the law.

Puffing with pride, Clara replied, "I do," and the sheriff fumbled in a drawer, fished out a deputy's badge, and handed it to her.

"Don't suppose I need to tell you that you're not legal without this badge?" the sheriff is supposed to have said.

"No, sir. I'll keep it with me all the time," the proud girl replied. Bolting out the door, she called her thanks over her shoulder.

The sheriff was probably still shaking his head as she rode away.

For days after bullying the sheriff into deputizing her, Clara rode out on the prairie accompanied by a vaquero, senses alert. Finally, on a long ride one day, she rode out in one direction but decided to return to the ranch by a different route. Entering a bank of low trees, she saw the outline of a riverbank up ahead. Riding closer, she detected a thin column of smoke. Thinking it was probably a party of her father's men, she rode up to get a better view.

According to Clara's version of events, below her, crouching over a fire they had built, were two Mexicans, described as "villainous-looking fellows." Their rifles lay nearby. The men were so absorbed in their cooking that they didn't see Clara approach.

Clara's smelled cooking meat, and she saw the carcass of one of her father's yearling calves nearby. Quickly, she decided that the men must be the cattle rustlers. She also suspected that these were the men who had murdered her friend, the foreman. Knowing that if that was so, they might kill her too, she decided it was still her duty as a deputy sheriff to arrest them. She motioned her attendant away, an order followed only reluctantly.

According to the story, Clara spurred her horse and dashed through the trees and over the riverbank, her carbine drawn and ready. The men, taken by surprise, threw up their hands. Speaking in Spanish, she ordered them to move away from the fire. Then she collected their rifles.

Because they appeared to be desperately hungry, she allowed the two men to finish their roasting. One of her friends declared later that she even ate with them. Clara never denied it, saying she didn't see why she shouldn't, since it was her father's steer they were cooking.

After eating, the deputy sheriff mounted her mustang and, with the help of her cowboy attendant, marched the men back to the Palo Alto ranch, where they were secured until a Ranger took charge and saw them safely to a Corpus Christi jail, according to Clara's interview for *World Magazine.*

The story of Clara's capture of rustlers is perhaps apocryphal—or it occurred on a visit to the ranch after she'd left to pursue her education. If, as sources say, she was eleven when her mother took her to New York, it's hard to imagine a girl that age capturing two rough desperadoes. But then again, Clara's feats were always larger than life—at least her stories of them were.

Clara's mother, Julia, was an attractive woman whose principal interests were her family and household. She oversaw her children's early education at the ranch and then sent Robert to private schools in San

Antonio. According to Martha Anne Turner's biography of Clara, in 1892 Julia Driscoll took her daughter to Europe to study; Clara was just eleven years old. She studied in France until she completed the equivalent of a high school education. Then she and her mother traveled extensively, even living briefly on a houseboat on the Godavari River in Bombay, India. Clara herself told the story of living in Spain when the Spanish-American War broke out in 1898. She remained there living as a Spanish woman with a Spanish name. Her dark hair and eyes and her fluency in Spanish allowed her to get away with this deception.

Clara Driscoll had learned from the best of both worlds—her intellect was supported by an outstanding education and the polish and sophistication of European travel combined with a thorough knowledge of ranch life and the South Texas landscape.

In 1900 mother and daughter were in London, preparing to sail for home, when Julia Fox Driscoll became ill and died unexpectedly. Her death was a great loss to Clara; the two had been so close for so many years. Shortly after Julia's death, Robert Driscoll had a mausoleum constructed at the Alamo Masonic Cemetery in San Antonio. There were four vaults, one for each member of his family, and Julia was the first occupant.

From her immersion in European culture—far older societies and customs than America's—Clara had developed an appreciation for Old World relics and antiquities. Back in Texas, however, she was surprised to find many of her fellow Texans were indifferent to the crumbling ruins of the aging missions that comprised her beloved state's history. Research had made her aware that the Alamo was internationally famous, and once back in San Antonio, she was appalled at its shabby state. She probably thought of the horror European tourists would feel upon visiting a site so shoddily treated by its caretakers. Although her ranch home was closer to Corpus Christi, Clara often visited San Antonio, a city where her family had close ties, including the mausoleum that held her mother's remains. She wrote the *San Antonio Express* a long letter expressing her concern about the "hideous" buildings surrounding the Alamo. The letter was published January 14, 1901.

Calling the Alamo a "silent monument of the dark and stormy days of Texas," she wrote:

> *How can we expect others to attach the importance to it that it so well deserves, when we Texans, who live within its shadow, are so careless of its existence? . . . Today the Alamo should stand out, free and clear. All the unsightly obstructions should be torn away. I am sure that if the matter were taken up by some patriotic Texans a sufficient amount could be raised that would enable something of the kind to be done.*

Although she claimed to miss the Mexican stands selling *dulces* and the chili queens who had long since been driven from the city's plazas, Clara was particularly distressed by the long barracks, its walls plastered with signs and billboards. She bemoaned the modernization of the structure and the encroaching commercial buildings. She wanted to keep the "foreign" element—the details of Spanish architecture—from disappearing from the site because she felt that attracted tourists. According to her long public letter, Clara said visitors to the site had asked incredulously, "Is that the Alamo?" They expected a larger and grander sight than the rather small, deteriorating mission buildings. Clara expected her letter and her interest to make an enterprising Texan take hold of the project, apparently not suspecting she would be that enterprising Texan. At the time she wrote this letter, Clara was not yet a member of the Daughters of the Texas Revolution. She joined in 1903.

The Alamo Mission

It is impossible to generalize about Texas terrain or landscape, since the state varies from the low, moist Gulf Coast region to the mountains of Big Bend, with semi-arid plains between much of those extremes. Friars coming to Mission San Antonio de Valero would have found themselves between the moist, humid climate of East Texas and the dry plains to the west. The terrain was grasslands, with occasional wooded areas. Some claim the shortened name, Alamo, was given to the mission because of a clump of cottonwood trees (*alamo* in Spanish) nearby. Others claim it was because the Alamo de Parra military company was briefly stationed there in the early 1800s to quell any uprisings in the San Antonio area supporting the Mexican move for independence. The men of the Spanish cavalry unit were from the village of Alamo in Mexico, and locals soon attached that name to the site. By the time of the battle, not many, even in San Antonio, knew the mission's proper name.

Established in 1718 by Father Olivares, the mission was the first mission on San Antonio River, first located on the west side of the river and then moved to its present location on the east side. For the Spanish, it provided a way station for travelers going from the Rio Grande to the missions in East Texas. Missions were named after saints, and this one was no exception. It was named in honor of its patron, St. Anthony of Padua, and in recognition of the Marquis de Valero, who was viceroy of New Spain at the time. The mission chapel and its surrounding buildings at one time covered almost three acres of land with quarters for the priests, soldiers, and natives along with a granary and a workhouse.

The first buildings were no doubt constructed of grass or perhaps wood. The first permanent building consisted of blocks of limestone or native chalk stone and was erected in 1727. Work on the chapel, also a building of limestone blocks, was begun in 1744. The story goes that by then the Indians at the Alamo were aware of other missions being established with churches on the grounds. The native peoples, newly converted to Christianity, clamored for a church, and construction was begun on the chapel building, which was originally designed to have two towers, a dome, and an elaborate façade. As it was being built, however, the entire thing collapsed. Some blamed this debacle on faulty design; others blamed the builders—mostly the Native Americans. After the collapse of the structure, an epidemic decimated the mission's Indian population, and the chapel was never completed.

At its peak, the mission consisted of the chapel on the east side of the complex, the adjoining long barracks—a convent space used for housing—the low barracks or south barracks, a main entrance protected by a parapet constructed of hides and earth, several small adobe huts on the west and north side, and a plaza in the center, all surrounded by a twelve-foot stone wall. The long barracks was a fifty-foot-long, two-story stone building with galleries above and below and many doors to the plaza. The rooms in the barracks were loop-holed for defense with rifles.

Chapter Four

Back in Texas

After her mother's unexpected death and her own brief return to Texas, Clara again left the United States to travel extensively in Europe, taking her close friend Florence Eager. She was gone for more than two years before returning to Texas more or less permanently in 1903. Unlike Adina, who was largely content to travel within Texas and the Southwest, Clara burned to see the world. In her lifetime she made fourteen crossings of the Atlantic, but she always returned to Texas and often stayed at San Antonio's Menger Hotel. As fate would have it, she was staying at the hotel on the day that Adina De Zavala was desperate for money.

Clara and Adina shared a Texas heritage, including deep familial roots that predated the revolution, and a love for the state and its history, but beyond that the two women could not have been more different. Clara was the taller of the two, slim, nearly always fashionably dressed in a flared skirt and a soft bodice embellished with tucks, her hair neatly piled atop her head and held with au courant combs. There is some debate about the color of her hair—descriptions of her range from dark to fair but in photographs it always appeared to be fairly dark. That fateful day at the Menger, Clara's cool, urbane sophistication and ease were in stark contrast to the fairly frantic Adina, with her wrinkled shirtwaist and crumped skirt, hair windblown, face red from exertion and desperation. Clara Driscoll was not unprepared to entertain Adina's request nor was she unfamiliar with the problem posed by the condition of the Alamo buildings. Still, the knock on her door surprised her.

The two women came from two different worlds in a city that was increasingly divided along racial lines. Adina's parentage and last name identified her as belonging to one side of the line, even though her skin was just as fair as Clara's, thanks to her Irish mother. But the division that existed and had grown between Anglos and Hispanics since the early nineteenth century saw the beginning of Anglo settlement in what was then Coahuila y Tejas. The Anglos who moved into the Mexican territory probably did not see themselves as part of a national movement, but they were strong examples of Manifest Destiny. As far as Americans were concerned, the occupation and civilization of new lands was considered a right, with little to no thought for the native populations that were displaced. For those coming to Texas, particularly under the *empresario* system, the native population, including both indigenous peoples and Mexicans of Spanish descent, represented nothing more than a small problem to overcome.

Prior to 1820, Spain had offered land to immigrants only under strict conditions, such as conversion to Catholicism. After Mexico gained its independence, it relaxed the restrictions; the law declared that a man could apply for land if he swore to recruit settlers to live on and develop that land. Mexico hoped to populate the vast northern reaches of its country, land heretofore undeveloped. Anglos from the United States received the vast majority of those land grants, earning the moniker *empresario* from the Mexicans. Moses Austin was the first *empresario*, actually receiving his grant from Spain, but he died before he could establish his colony. It was left to his son, Stephen F. Austin, to establish Austin's Colony in Central Texas. The younger Austin served Texas so admirably, especially in negotiations with Mexico City, in which he took a more moderate position of reason compared to some of his hotter colleagues, that he became known as the Father of Texas. Still hoping for good relations with Mexico, Austin did not support the Texas Declaration of Independence. Robertson's Colony, with headquarters in the Salado area, was established by another Anglo, Sterling Robertson, and was one of the larger and more important colonies. Interestingly, Martín de Leon was the only man of Hispanic descent granted land under the *empresario* system.

The effects of this kind of migration on native populations are well documented, though we may never appreciate the full devastation to peoples and cultures. The racial divisions that developed in the Mexican territory that became the Republic of Texas and then the State of Texas displayed textbook examples of the stratification and segregation common in such migration patterns. From the earliest days of the land grants, the Anglo settlers who moved into the region, often called Texians, considered themselves superior to the native Mexican population. The slaughters ordered by Santa Anna, most notably at the Alamo and Goliad, added flaming fuel to the smoldering fire, because Texians tarred all Mexicans with the brush of the cruelty ordered by Santa Anna. As the years after the battle passed, the separation between Anglos and Mexicans increased. Mexicans were regarded as "less"—corrupt, lazy, superstitious (mostly because of their strong Catholic faith), uneducated, and even unclean. After Texas gained its independence from Mexico and then joined the United States, as the white-centric culture developed, a white power structure emerged. Compounding the political stratification of Texas society was rapid commercialization, especially in urban areas like San Antonio. Socioeconomic status and material opportunities—both of which were most readily available to Anglos—became the measures of a man and his family.

With three grandparents of Anglo descent and her own fair skin and blue eyes, Adina De Zavala never identified with the Mexican population in Texas. In fact, she despised the then-current designation of American Mexican. She was, however, fiercely proud of her Grandfather de Zavala, and since she bore his last name, she was often viewed as "other" by the invading Anglo population. As far as "high society" was concerned, she could never quite equal the status of someone like Clara Driscoll, whose family was part of the power structure, by virtue of their wealth and landholdings.

The differences between them were not on the minds of either woman on the day Adina pounded on Clara's door at the Menger Hotel. In Adina, Clara probably didn't recognize the "enterprising, patriotic Texan" she had called for in her letter to the newspaper any more than she'd envisioned herself as the donor destined to save the Alamo. But eyeing the distraught woman at her door, Clara heard the determination in her voice, saw the sparkle in her eye, and was intrigued by her request for help.

Clara opened the door more widely and beckoned Adina in. "Won't you come in? I was just about to have tea, and I would be pleased if you would join me." An English tea set, complete with a bowl of cubed sugars and a plate of dainty cakes, was on a low table in front of a velveteen settee.

As the two women sat, Clara—ever the sophisticate—said, "I prefer my tea the British way, with milk, not cream."

Adina didn't care about the tea. She was after money. And she entered the large suite with a slight sense of awe. The sitting room was done in tones of a dull mauve, which were rather depressing, but several vases of fresh flowers brightened the space. French doors opened onto a small balcony overlooking the plaza and let in a bit of welcome fresh air.

When Clara handed her a cup and saucer, Adina started to relax, just a bit. She took the beverage with a steady hand, in spite of her inner turmoil.

"Tell me the story," Clara said, sipping the hot tea.

Adina launched into the tale with her usual enthusiasm for her sub-ject. She explained the situation to Clara, "There's this hotel company that's ready to buy the property where Mission San Antonio de Valero sits. Well, it's not the mission itself, that building was destroyed years ago. But the long barracks. Anyway, the Hugo and Schmeltzer grocery firm owns the barracks, but they're considering selling it to a hotel com-pany that has this plan to tear the whole thing down and build a hotel and liquor store there, instead! And, I just can't let that happen!"

Clara eyed Adina with a bit more respect than when she originally arrived at her door. "Of course not," she replied. "A hotel and liquor store would be a terrible distraction for visitors. It would take away the glory of the Alamo. But that terribly ugly building to the northwest must come down. It's so unsightly with that wooden frame around it and those posters and things plastered all over the walls. The chapel must stand in solitary splendor."

Adina must have squirmed on the uncomfortable settee, but she did not say what was on her mind. The building that Clara found so unat-tractive was the long barracks. That structure was the historic part—the part she most wanted to conserve. It was where the Texians fought and died while women and children were sheltered in the chapel building. The chapel was not the scene of the fighting and deaths, and in fact the City of San Antonio already owned that building. Still Adina kept her mouth shut. She needed Clara's money, and now was not the time to quarrel. If Clara would buy the barracks—regardless of her intentions or understanding of history—the building might yet be preserved.

"So just what did you have in mind?" Clara asked.

Adina explained the reason for her presence at the hotel that day. "I was going to ask the Kampmanns—they own this hotel—to help me buy the property, but I've just missed them. They left this morning for Europe. But I understand you're also a woman of means, and I'm pray-ing you could find it in your heart to help save the mission. You're my

View of Alamo Plaza from the southwest. Library of Congress, Historic American Building Survey, April 1938. Arthur W. Stewart, photographer.

last idea. If you won't help, this sacred site will be lost to the generations who come after us."

Clara carefully placed her teacup on its china saucer, pursed her lips, and looked across the table at Adina for a long, quiet moment, not saying anything. Adina felt like a century passed as Clara sat there, weighing the gravity of the situation Adina had presented. After what seemed an eternity to Adina but was probably only a few seconds, Clara said, "I'm really your last hope?"

"Yes," Adina said, "if you won't come to its rescue, I fear by this time next year, the mission will be no more."

"In that case," Clara said decisively, "I'll do it. How much do you suppose it would take to save the mission from commercial enterprise?"

Adina's posture sagged with relief. "Really, you mean it?" she asked.

She explained the financials to Clara as she understood them. "I'm not sure as of today, but Mr. Schmeltzer has talked to me of a price of $75,000. Perhaps a $5,000 down payment would secure the property until the Daughters of the Republic can raise the necessary money to complete the purchase. I'm the president of the De Zavala Daughters, and I know they can raise the money. If you could see your way clear to pay the down payment, we would be so grateful."

Clara stood and smoothed the barely perceptible wrinkles from her tidy skirt, "Let's go see Mr.—what was his name?'"

With a great sigh of relief, Adina supplied, "Schmeltzer."

The story of what happened that day is disputed by some historians. In later years, the DRT's official account of the events stated that Clara made the connection with Gustav Schmeltzer on her own and left Pompeo Coppini and Adina De Zavala completely out of the story. Since Adina had the connection with the grocer, it seems more likely that the two women went to that initial meeting together. Gustav Schmeltzer would later issue a notarized statement that included the fact that Adina had contacted him as early as 1892 about the building, a statement that all but confirms the two women approached him together. About the time of Adina's approach to her, Clara joined the DRT, probably expressly because of her concern about the Alamo.

Since Adina's original approach to the grocer about the property in the early 1890s, Gustav Schmeltzer had treated her with courtesy and a respect not always shown women in business transactions in that day, especially women of Mexican descent. After all, in 1903 women were still seventeen years away from having the vote, and who knew if a Mexican woman, descendant of a hero or not, would ever be allowed the franchise. In addition, Schmeltzer had no idea where the woman thought she might raise the money for the purchase, but he apparently was a gentleman and treated her request seriously.

When Adina introduced Clara as someone interested, with her, in the purchase of the property, he treated the matter with due respect.

Mr. Hugo, Mr. Schmeltzer, and the other owners of the property once again offered the women their best price. Agreeing to "contribute" $10,000 to the cause, they indicated that the final sales price would be

$75,000.[7] They expected a $5,000 deposit and an additional $4,500 after thirty days to extend the option for one year. At that time, according to author Gale Hamilton Shiffrin in *Women of the Alamo*, the entire down payment of $25,000 would be due, with arrangements made for payment of the balance.

Clara wrote a check for $5,000, and the two women left, confident that they could raise the necessary funds.

Clara and Adina had committed the DRT chapter to a huge debt, much beyond anything the efforts of the De Zavala Daughters could hope to raise quickly. The DRT at large formed a commission to raise the funds, with Clara as the chair and Adina as a member. Over the year, the group sent out letters to Texans throughout the state. Each recipient was asked to donate fifty cents and to pass the request to a friend. But a few days before the $25,000 was due, the committee had raised only a little over a thousand dollars. The hotel syndicate Coppini had mentioned was still negotiating to buy the property, confident that the women would fail to raise the money.

When their efforts to raise private funds stalled, Adina and Clara formed a plan to get state support for their efforts. It is unclear whether Adina or Clara first appealed to the legislature for the funds to buy the building. Some sources say Adina submitted a bill, on behalf of the De Zavala chapter, to the legislature. But there is also a record of Clara appearing before the legislature in the company of a Mrs. R. A. Coleman in a meeting that excluded Adina. Regardless, the DRT offered to give the State of Texas clear title to the property and to turn over any monies so far collected if the legislature allocated the funds. The DRT also promised to maintain the property as a hall of fame and museum of history in memory of the fallen heroes of the Alamo. No matter who made that first appeal, in 1904 both houses of the legislature approved the sum of $5,000 for the DRT finance committee to use as part of the next payment on the property. Elation soon gave way to despair, however, when

Governor S.W.T. Lanham refused to sign the bill on the grounds it was not proper use of taxpayer money. With that avenue closed to the group, Clara Driscoll again stepped in, paying the balance of the down payment due in February 1904. In addition, after complicated negotiations involving her lawyers and Hugo and Schmeltzer, she signed a note to pay $10,000 annually for the next four years, at 6 percent per annum. She obligated herself for $50,000 plus interest, taxes, and insurance. The DRT was obligated to come up with the balance of the purchase price to repay Clara Driscoll, but she was firmly in the driver's seat.

Clara required that the deed for the property be made out to the Daughters of the Republic of Texas, not to the De Zavala chapter, a fact that Adina would later regret. At the moment it seemed that the crisis was behind them. The Alamo would be saved. Clara Driscoll became a heroine overnight. Texans were amazed and intrigued by a young woman paying that much money for a pile of crumbling bricks, no matter its historical significance. The attitude toward saving the Alamo changed rapidly and dramatically, and Texans took pride in Clara and her action. Unfortunately, Adina got little of the credit.

Interestingly, fund-raising became much easier as people responded to the story of Clara paying all that money to save the Alamo property from development. The DRT set up collection booths outside the Alamo, and funds from the 1904 Fiesta—San Antonio's annual grand celebration, which Clara presided over, went to save the Alamo. The DRT had moved its cause from reliance on asking its membership and schoolchildren for nickels and dimes to high-society events. Still, they had raised only slightly over $5,000 by February 1904.

Clara's gesture—her grand financial contribution—was neither anonymous nor unnoticed. Various patriotic groups petitioned the legislature to repay Miss Driscoll in full. Finally, representatives of both houses asked to meet with a committee member from the DRT. Naturally the DRT sent Clara.

Slim and young, then only twenty-five, Clara poured out her passion for Texas history and its monuments to that stern body of men in January 1905. When she finished her presentation, Samuel Early Johnson,[8] proposed a bill appropriating the money to reimburse her and the Twenty-Ninth Legislature of Texas accepted it. The appropriation was not completely without controversy. Some legislators objected that it was entirely too much money to spend on a crumbling pile of mortar, and they saw no equivalent financial return for the economy. Clara's argument that the past would inspire the future did not impress them. When an amendment was proposed that would have put control of the property in the hands of a gubernatorial commission, Clara insisted the DRT retain control of the property. Otherwise, the DRT would turn down the proposed funding.

Eventually, the bill passed both houses and was signed by the governor in January 1905. Later that year, the governor formally gave control of the property to the DRT. In San Antonio, that meant Adina's chapter—the De Zavala Daughters, would be the custodians. Adina couldn't have been happier, but her happiness would be short-lived. She would soon realize that she should have specified that full control of the Alamo property should be retained by the De Zavala chapter of the DRT and not by the organization as a whole.

Still, two Irish American women, with ancestors who had served at San Jacinto, had saved the Alamo. Adina De Zavala had realized her goal—for the moment—of preserving the long barracks and stopping further commercial development. Clara Driscoll became known as the Savior of the Alamo. The story should have ended there, but it didn't.

The Daughters of the Republic of Texas

The DRT is the oldest patriotic organization in Texas, and one of the oldest in the nation. Soon after its founding, it had chapters in several Texas cities. Although the De Zavala Daughters' founding predated the DRT, they were not considered the oldest chapter. That honor went to Galveston's Sidney Sherman chapter, followed by the San Jacinto chapter in Houston. Mrs. Anson Jones, the widow of the last president of the Republic of Texas, was president of the DRT when the De Zavala group joined, but Adina remained in firm control of the De Zavala chapter. Later, however, Adina made the group an auxiliary of the DRT, rather than a full chapter, so they could admit members who did not meet the strict DRT qualifications, which included being personally acceptable to the DRT and a descendant of a man or woman who rendered loyal service to the Republic prior to annexation on February 19, 1846. Applicants were required to provide documentation of their ancestry; acceptable ancestors included recipients of land grants, either from Stephen F. Austin in Austin's Colony or other land grants before 1836 when all public lands were declared the property of the Republic. Many land grants went to veterans of the Texas War of Independence but apparently being descended from a loyal resident, with emphasis on loyalty, or from an officer in service of the Republic counted.

CHAPTER FIVE

---•●•---

Fiction and Real Romance

A slender woman with light brown hair and eyes stepped into a horse carriage decked with garlands of roses. She wore a soft rose-colored gown with ruffled sleeves, a ruffled neckline, and lace panels inset in the long, flowing skirt which had a slight train that she held up with one white-gloved hand. In the other hand, she held a parasol matching her dress. Pinned to the slightly scooped neckline of her dress was a boutonniere of roses and on her head, a tiara. She was the Queen of the San Antonio Fiesta. The date was April, probably 1905, and Clara Driscoll, "Savior of the Alamo," had been chosen for the prestigious role.

Several other women were seated in the carriage with her, all waving at the spectators as they approached the Alamo Plaza. Once the carriage reached the Alamo, it stopped, and Queen Clara threw the first rose. The Battle of the Flowers had begun.

San Antonio Fiesta—the biggest citywide event of the year—had begun in 1896, on the fiftieth anniversary of the Battle of San Jacinto, which it commemorates. The festival, known today as the high-society event Fiesta San Antonio, was begun by women who decorated carriages, baby buggies, and bicycles with live flowers, parading their creations through the city to the Alamo Plaza, where they gathered in front

Clara Driscoll. The flowers in her hair may indicate that this photo was taken when she was Fiesta Queen, probably 1905. DRT Collection at Texas A&M University-San Antonio.

of the Alamo buildings and pelted each other with flowers. It was called the Battle of the Flowers.[9]

On that April evening, Clara would have abandoned the parasol in favor of a rose-colored fan decorated with feathers, chosen to match her dress. Clara would go on to reign for three years as Fiesta Queen, most certainly a tribute to her reputation as the Savior of the Alamo.

No doubt Henry Hulme (Hal) Sevier was among the crowd watching the parade and flowery battle during that first year of Clara's reign. Hal, a transplant to Texas and a freshman in the Texas legislature, had met Clara previously and had been entranced by her appearance before that august body to ask for reimbursement of her funds spent to save the Alamo. Sevier believed in Clara's assertion that the past would inform the future, perhaps less out of logic than out of admiration for the young woman. When friends introduced them outside the legislature, there was a quick attraction on both sides, and they were soon considered a twosome.

Sevier's ancestry included close ties to Spanish and French royalty, veterans of the Revolutionary War, and a mother who had been born in the Republic of Texas. John Sevier, one of Hal's ancestors, was a frontier pioneer, leading settlers into Tennessee's Cumberland Valley. A fierce Indian fighter, he was known as the hero of the Battle of King's Mountain. Hal Sevier is said to have resembled this relative and also to have been an extraordinarily handsome man.

As a youth, Sevier received a classical education; his father was president of the University of the South at Sewanee, Tennessee. Sevier began his career as the editor of a country newspaper, and by the early 1900s had moved to Sabinal, Uvalde County, Texas, where he published the weekly *Sabinal Sentinel* and from where he was elected to the legislature. He served two terms, but by the end of his second term, in 1906, he had been named financial editor of the *New York Sun* and was preparing to move to the Empire State.

By the time Sevier took the post at the *Sun*, Clara had already moved to New York to begin a writing career. Perhaps because of her career ambitions, theirs was not a fast-moving courtship. From the time in 1905 when he first met Clara at the Texas State Capitol Building, it would be three years before they married.

Clara Driscoll embedded many of her own beliefs and prejudices in her writing. In fact, the attitudes that would influence her strong stand on how the Alamo should be developed and preserved and her relationships with the DRT are revealed in her three major literary works: a novel, *The Girl from La Gloria*; a collection of short stories, *In the Shadow of the Alamo*; and a musical comedy, *Mexicana*.

Clara was not a novice writer. In addition to her impassioned pleas to the newspaper regarding historic preservation, Clara Driscoll had written numerous travel articles over the years, inspired by her travels with her mother. After she had taken her stand to save the Alamo with her checkbook and she was assured by legislative action that the Alamo was safe from commercial development, she decided to explore other aspects of life, and she turned to fiction. Certainly, her extensive education gave her a background in literature and equipped her to be a writer. She may well have been influenced by novels by other Texas women, or she may have simply wanted to try her hand.

It would be easy to dismiss Clara's first novel, *The Girl from La Gloria*, as one of a spate of ranch romances that appeared in the early twentieth century. It is indeed not a great novel, but it is also not without interesting points and conflicts, some of which reflect Clara's heritage and her absorption in Texas history and culture. But some of the book is downright puzzling.

The elements of a romance novel are all there—star-crossed lovers, more than one villain, a tragic ending. In some senses the novel is autobiographical, and it is fairly easy to equate the fictional characters with real persons in Clara's life. The empire-building rancher, Edward

Benton, is clearly an only-slightly-disguised version of Clara's father, whom she admired unquestioningly. As owner of the Calaveras spread, Benton holds title to vast lands to which he has no legal claim, and as the novel unfolds, Benton's voracious land-grabbing troubles neither the author nor her fictional counterpart. It is revealed that much of Benton's huge ranch, now fenced, once belonged to Manuel Rodriguez, a man who Benton murdered. Adding to the drama is the fact that there is more than one villain, including a scheming lawyer and a guardian who would marry his ward in order to control her fortune.

At the center of the novel is the young and beautiful Ilaria Buckley, the child of a wastrel Anglo father and a passive Mexicana mother, Concha Rodriguez. Concha was the daughter of the murdered Manuel. As the novel opens, Ilaria is in a convent in Corpus Christi where she has been schooled for eight years. Without permission, she leaves and returns to La Gloria, where the remaining small bit of Rodriguez lands are, and to Paula, the aged Mexicana woman who has cared for her all her life.

When Randor Walton, the son of Benton's New York partner, loses his way on the prairie during a visit to the ranch, he finds himself at La Gloria. Randor is described in the novel as unusually good-looking. Paula, after seeing him, exclaims, "*Dioscitos*, that a man should be so beautiful!" It is doubtless no coincidence that Hal Sevier, the object of Clara's affections, was consistently described as an unusually good-looking man.

Predictably, Randor and Ilaria fall in love at first sight. After several visits, he asks her to marry him, but the road to romance is not smooth for the lovers. Ilaria's uncle, who claims to be her guardian, wants to marry her even though she despises him. Benton's lawyer, oddly named Heathhaven, schemes to "represent" her in recovery of the land the Rodriguez family had lost to Benton so that he can make a fortune off both Ilaria and Benton. The intrigue is almost too complicated to follow.

Clara's handling of race is perhaps the most interesting aspect of the novel. She introduces the subject this way, "In this land of cattle and mesquite, two names held prominence through the alternating periods of prosperity and decay: Benton and Rodriguez, types of opposing races; one, descendant from the Anglo Saxon; the other, from the darker skinned aborigines of old Mexico." Clara was writing of life as she knew it on the range and in Texas, where most ranch land had originally been held by Tejanos and then had been transferred—legally or often not—to Anglo hands. Racism, as she knew and absorbed it, mostly involved Anglo discrimination against Mexicans. Over a half century after the fall of the Alamo, Texan resentment of Mexicans still rang strong. The two races developed distinct communities, and romance could easily go awry when young people attempted to break those barriers. Anti-Catholic sentiments were also strong among the Anglo settlers, and these sentiments, like race relations, are a source of conflict in much of Driscoll's fiction.

Throughout *La Gloria*, Mexicans are routinely referred to as "greasers" and are scorned for their indolence, greed, and superstition. Despite her devotion to Paula and her own heritage, Ilaria never identifies as Mexicana, which may be another indication of the autobiographical aspect of this heroine. Clara could identify with a star-struck lover, but not with a Tejano. At one point Ilaria decries a Mexican horse wrangler who has been loyal to her all his life because she believes he has accepted a bribe to kill her Anglo lover.

"No wonder Americans scorn you Mexicans," she screams. "You would sell your soul for money!"

And when an Anglo woman, with her eye on Randor, taunts Ilaria that Randor cannot seriously love her because she is Mexican, she believes it and says sadly to her lover that she is "not of his people." Unwittingly, Clara may have expressed, through Ilaria, some of the emotions felt by her fellow DRT member, Adina De Zavala.

Ilaria's attitude toward the lands stolen from her family is unexpected but also telling of Clara's attitudes. On more than one occasion, she does not blame the Anglo who took the land but says it is the Mexican's fault for losing it. This attitude seems contradictory for the fictional heroine, but it might fit with Clara's interpretation of the importance of the Alamo. She saw it as a shrine to brave Anglo defenders, overlooking the Mexicans who fought with Travis and giving not a second thought to members of Santa Anna's army.

Where Clara displayed real talent in her writing was in her description of the borderlands, the animals, the moods of the landscape, and the lives both of wealthy ranchers and vaqueros. It was a life she knew well since much of her formative early life was spent on a ranch, and rather than being sheltered in the ranch house, she took part in ranch life. Indeed, Perdito, the loyal but fractious pony of the novel, is probably named after the pet wildcat she had as a girl. Clara knew and loved the land, and she capably caught it on paper, portraying the ranch house, the cattle drive, the peon's *jacal*, even the *arroyo* which figures prominently and tragically in the tale.

The Girl from La Gloria was met with some critical acclaim, but it was also well publicized that the author was the "Savior of the Alamo." How much her literary reputation rested on her connection to the Alamo and how much on her skill as a writer is a question to be begged. G. P. Putnam's Sons, however, expected great things of *The Girl from La Gloria* and urged their new young author to follow quickly with another manuscript. Soon she sent them a collection of short stories titled *In the Shadow of the Alamo*. The work clearly reflected Driscoll's passion for Texas history and her firm beliefs about the importance of the Alamo story. With a couple of exceptions—one set in a military camp and another about a chili queen in San Antonio's old Military Plaza—the tales are set in missions in the San Antonio area.

The first story, "The Custodian of the Alamo," clearly delineates Clara's passion for the Alamo. The first section traces the history of events leading to the battle, the battle itself, and the subsequent decay of the chapel and surrounding structures. In the second part, romance is still—or again—on Clara's mind. The central figure is a young, attractive woman. A stranger, handsome of course, wanders in seeking souvenirs and proves a willing audience for her history lessons. The ending is a bit abrupt—he leaves, returns, declares his love, and says she must come away with him. In an answer that perhaps foretells Clara's ultimate answer to Sevier and move to New York, the young woman agrees. Romanticism triumphs.

There's lots of instant love in these pages. Young people are smitten with a single look. Usually the male is Anglo, an outsider, from the north, and the girl, a Tejano. The young man is struck by her dark looks—brown skin, eyes like deep pools, wild and free hair. After a few brief encounters, the young man often asks the girl to go away with him, and she agrees without hesitation. But there are no happy endings—one or the other of the lovers dies, or in the case of the chili queen, the girl's Mexican lover has too strong a hold over her and at the last minute she goes away with him instead of the new romantic interest. Love is destined to bring tragedy in the Driscoll canon.

In at least two stories, "Sister Genevieve" and "The Old Priest of San Francisco de la Espada," characters are caught between their commitments to the church and the longings of their hearts. This may reflect Clara's own conflict. Raised a Catholic, she knew how strict the church was about matters of the heart when they crossed vows of commitment to the church. And she was harboring romantic ideas about love. In these stories, it's not difficult to tell that Clara's sympathies—or dramatic sense—lay with the thwarted lovers. In "Sister Genevieve," a young nun, convent educated, has taken her vows and committed herself to Christ because the man she desperately loves is married. Having done so, she withers away—perhaps from tuberculosis. Her lover comes for her, tells her his wife is dead (Clara seems to have no moral difficulty with this solution to the problem), but she dies in his arms. As Randor comes too late to save Ilaria from the *arroyo*, this lover is also too late to save her.

In "The Old Priest of San Francisco de la Espada," an elderly priest apparently took his vows as a youth after the death of his lover. Now, old and frail, he finds a piece of ribbon that convinces him his beloved Helen has come back. Too soon, he realizes it is an apparition. "And though Father Gilot died wearing the cassock of one whose life was consecrated to God, and with a prayer in his soul, he clasped in his hand a knot of blue ribbon, and in his heart was enshrined the image of a woman's face."

Clara Driscoll followed these highly romanticized, tragic stories with an abrupt change of tone—writing and producing the comic opera *Mexicana*. She wrote the work because, as she said, librettists searched the world for exotic settings for their productions, but none had considered Mexico. She was familiar with the country and, despite her literary stereotyping, had admiration for its people. Raymond Hubbell, one of America's foremost composers, best known for "Poor Butterfly," was her coauthor on *Mexicana*, and either Clara or her brother Robert financed this dramatic production's eighty-two-performance run in New York's Lyric Theater.[10] The Shuberts, producers of the musical, had a show-business name that carried some weight even in the early 1900s. The show featured lyrics by Robert B. Smith, and Clara spared no expense in sets and costumes. Every effort was taken to assemble the perfect cast, an assignment complicated by the fact that the chorus girls were all to be convincing as either Mexican or Native American. No blondes need apply. Great care was taken throughout in order to introduce New York audiences to an authentic version of the colorful culture of a Mexican village—including flowers, bright costumes, and a leisurely pace of life. Playing on the well-accepted stereotype of Mexicans as lazy, one critic wrote that the play brought to life the "lethargy of the Mexican" because Mexicans and Indians in costume displayed the culture's reverence for *mañana* or tomorrow. Far from being lethargic, however, the show was full of color, action, and music, its opening scene showing a typical Mexican market with pottery, flowers, and country produce.

Like most of Clara's writing, this production features an outsider, a speculator from the north who goes bankrupt when he tries to manage a Mexican mine, where workers counter his ambition with the philosophy of *mañana*. Ultimately the interloper masquerades as a bandit. Predictably, he falls in love with Mexicana, the most beautiful of the Mexican maidens. The story offers Clara's usual treatment of romance but without the tragic ending. Also, having set the production in Mexico, she treats the people and their culture much more sympathetically than in her fiction.

By the time *Mexicana* had finished its run at the Lyric and gone on tour, Clara was apparently ready to acknowledge Hal Sevier's place in her life. And after a two-year "career" as a writer, perhaps Clara thought it time that she turned to other interests. Or perhaps having written so much about romance, Clara thought it time to act on the romance in her own life. By 1906, Sevier had served two terms in the Texas legislature and was living in New York and working at *The Sun*, a major New York City newspaper.

The two were married at high noon on July 31 in a small but fashionable wedding in St. Patrick's Cathedral in Manhattan. Dinner afterward was at the famous Delmonico's restaurant, where they no doubt dined on Delmonico steaks and chose from what was claimed to be the country's finest wine list. The wedding was widely covered in both San Antonio and New York City. Reporters in both cities called it "the romance of the Alamo" and made note of the fact that as a legislator Sevier had supported Texas legislation to reimburse Miss Driscoll for the funds she had expended to save the Alamo and the long barracks. They no doubt chose New York for their nuptials, instead of Clara's beloved Texas, because they knew Sevier's work would require them to make their home there, at least for a few years.

Within weeks of the wedding, the couple embarked on a European tour, headed for England, France, and Italy. In their first-class suite on the SS *Amerika*, they found twelve bottles of champagne, fruit baskets, and flowers. Clara kept scrapbooks of the trip, filling them with memorabilia and pictures, postcards, and ticket stubs. There were souvenir programs from the Folies Bergère and a program from the Moulin Rouge. A special fan from Café de la Paix showed a cat holding a glass of champagne.

She wrote sprightly and forthright postcards to friends and family and entries in a memory book. "Even cross Bobby is always willing to open my trunks," she wrote after three days at sea. Note the plural of the word trunks. Clara no doubt traveled in high style.

Early in the honeymoon, however, Clara became concerned about Hal's drinking. On another page in her memory book she would write, "Six glasses a day."

In another instance, she chronicled Hal's champagne consumption:

WHAT A NIGHT
8:30 Marignlly [sic]
11:30 Bal Tabarin Champagne
1:30 a.m., Rat Mort, Champagne
5:30 still Rat Mort and more Champagne
6 a.m. Drin[ks]-5-the Halles Market
7 a.m. Filet de Sole Restaurant for breakfast
8 a.m.—back to Champagne—until 5 p.m. the next day

The Driscolls' large orders for alcoholic beverages to be delivered to various hotel suites suggest that they entertained widely. Clara remained concerned about her new husband's consumption of whiskey, throughout the trip, however.

After enjoying the night life in Paris, the theater in London, and the art and architecture in Italy, the couple was grateful to be back on

American shores at the end of October 1906, moving into an apartment on Madison Avenue.

Never one to be idle, Clara immediately undertook the project of building a grand home for them, on Long Island, near such neighbors as the Theodore Roosevelts. Clara had collected photographs from all over Europe of architectural features she found appealing—unusual entrances, formal gardens, statues, and the like. When finished, the Sevier house's stucco and terra-cotta exterior and tile roof perhaps harked back to Clara's love of all things Texan, but she incorporated details she had noted in Europe that particularly intrigued her, such as a courtyard that mimicked those she had seen in Italy.

She hired Charles L. Berg, an architect known for designing country houses that sat well on their landscape. Clara worked closely with Berg, specifying the long hall that ran the length of the two-wing residence, including a library and a conservatory for the books and music Clara loved. A terrace overlooked formal gardens and, beyond, a scenic ravine.

Like many a newlywed, Clara became devoted to cooking and gardening and apparently did much of that work herself, especially preparing meals. She frequently sat at her desk and leafed through a collection of recipes, most copies in longhand, others with notes and underlining she had added. The couple may have forsaken Texas for Manhattan for their wedding, but they kept their taste for simple Texas food—cornbread, biscuits, and stew. Clara brought some Mexican recipes from her ranch childhood, too, and was known for her chicken tamales. They also ate a lot of eggs—creamed, poached, scrambled, baked, and Clara's special Goldenrod Eggs, which featured mashed, hard-boiled eggs in white sauce on toast.

After the wedding, Clara did not entirely abandon her literary career for domestic bliss. Although little record remains of her output, she continued to write, usually stories much like those from *In the Shadow of the*

Alamo. She customarily wrote her stories and submitted them to editors in longhand.

Despite the fact that she was busy with entertaining, cooking, and gardening, and her literary efforts, Clara was homesick. She missed Texas, and she continued, long distance, to maintain her concern for preservation of Texas history and monuments. In truth, she also missed the Texas spirit and the camaraderie of her DRT sisters, with whom she maintained ties through occasional visits and correspondence.

While events were unfolding in Texas, Clara's homesickness for the Lone Star State would eventually lead her to take action in New York to bring a little Texas to her. Hal Sevier, though not a native Texan himself, had learned that she did whatever she set her mind to, so he was not surprised when one night as the couple sat in the comfortable parlor of their huge home, each reading, Clara looked up from her book and said, "Mr. Sevier, we need to gather together the Texas expatriates here in New York. I'm lonely for all things Texas."

Sevier, hidden behind a newspaper, replied, "I'll talk to some of the men."

Clara thought about this for a few minutes and then stood up decisively. "No," she said. "Not another men's organization. Women will run this one. But members must have been born in Texas or lived there for a number of years."

"Women will run this organization? Why?" Sevier asked as he put aside the newspaper.

Clara's answer harkened back to her DRT training: "Because we're the ones who preserve the landmarks. We care about everything about Texas—the history, the food, the way we lived. You men are at home anywhere. Look how easily you adjusted to living in New York."

"And you haven't?" Hal asked as he made an expansive gesture with his arm, indicating the luxury that surrounded them, each detail of which Clara had personally selected and supervised.

"No, and I never will," she said fiercely. "New York is a foreign country to me."

Hal Sevier wisely kept silent at that, but he was one of the first men to join the Texas Club as an associate member.

In a sense, Clara was extending the idea of the DRT to New York City. At the very least, she had learned some lessons for women and organizations and their power from her membership in the DRT.

Clara contacted Texas-born women she knew in the city and led the effort to organize the club. By 1911, the club was flourishing, with Clara as the president. One of her first projects would be a celebration of the Battle of San Jacinto, in New York City, a celebration that harked back to her days as Queen of Fiesta San Antonio.

Clara announced to a gathering of the women officers of the Texas Club, "We must mark the anniversary of Houston's victory at the Battle of San Jacinto. I propose we sponsor a ball at the Plaza Hotel on April 21."

"Let's have a reenactment of Santa Anna's surrender," one of the women suggested.

Clara, possibly a bit put out that she hadn't thought of it first, agreed, and the ladies chose a Texas menu, or at least they gave each dish a Texas name:

> *Oysters Port Lavaca*
> *Soup Mexico*
> *Radishes Olives Almonds*
> *Turbot Matagorda*
> *Lamb Goliad*
> *Potatoes San Patricio*
> *Lemon Ice Sarita*
> *Chicken Gonzales*
> *Salad San Jacinto*

Roast Glacé Tortoni
Petits Fours
Coffee

With Clara's help, no doubt financial as well as administrative, the club purchased a brownstone mansion in a fashionable part of Manhattan to serve as its headquarters. While the mansion was not a venue for the occasional lavish celebration that the club hosted and promoted, the home-like building served as a gathering point for Texans living in or visiting New York. If Adina De Zavala had ever visited the city, she would have been greeted at the club by Texans, probably Clara Driscoll Sevier herself, and offered a variety of Texas newspapers. The Texas Club fit perfectly with Clara's passion for preserving Texas history and landmarks. If she couldn't live in Texas, she would create a bit of Texas in New York.

During Clara's early years in New York, she and Adina had exchanged affectionate, friendly letters, discussing DRT business and various of their fellow members, including a DRT member's mother, a founder who was by then quite old and frail. Adina wrote Clara that she had assured the daughter of the venerable old lady that Clara possessed a true and patriotic spirit and would work toward the cause of preservation.

We don't know when Clara and Adina ever specifically discussed their disagreement about what preservation meant at the Alamo Plaza site. Clara would soon demonstrate—even from New York—that her intention to tear down the long barracks to make the area surrounding the chapel a beautiful garden of remembrance was still in full force. The letters between the two, however, plus the appeals for money Adina sent out, written in her own hand, clearly specified that the money requested was for the preservation of the building adjacent to the Alamo chapel, with the intention of making it a "worthy and artistic monument to the memory of those valiant martyrs who fell inside its walls."

Clara could not be called a pioneer in Texas women's literature. Women had been writing about their experiences in the state for almost a hundred years by the time Clara picked up her pen. Mary Austin Holley's memoir-like *Texas* (1833) was said to be the first book in English about Texas. Holley was a cousin of Stephen F. Austin, and her book describes a visit to Austin's Colony. Perhaps the first novel about Texas, by a woman, appeared in France in 1819 with a title that roughly translates as *A History of Texas, or the Voyage of Madame *** to the United States and Mexico*. The author was identified only by initials, and there is no record of personal experience qualifying her to write about a short-lived French colony on the Trinity River.

The Alamo had supplied subject matter for at least two novels. Augusta Evans Wilson's *Inez: A Tale of the Alamo* (1855) pits an Anglo heroine against the unscrupulous wiles of the Catholic priesthood, while Amelia E. Barr's *Remember the Alamo* (1888) is typical of the anti-Catholic feeling that marked much nineteenth-century Texas fiction.

Clara Driscoll may have been familiar with some novels set in the American West but outside Texas. Emerson Hough and Owen Wister, both masters of the ranch romance, burst onto the American literature scene only a year or two before Clara began writing fiction. She might even have read *Heart's Desire* or *The Virginian*.

Similarly, the life of Mary Hallock Foote, who gave up an artistic career in New York City to marry a miner and follow him to the wilds of Idaho and California, might have intrigued a Texas ranch girl familiar with New York. Clara also might have read Mary Hunter Austin, though she would not have been much in sympathy with Austin's fascination with Native American life in the Mojave Desert. Nor would she have sympathized with her feminism.

CHAPTER SIX

Adina's Daring Stand

The morning of February 10, 1908, dawned cold and dreary in San Antonio. Keys in hand, Adina De Zavala, dressed in her warmest clothes, showed up at the Alamo Plaza with a fierce determination in her eyes. As she crossed the grounds, she only glanced at the nearby construction equipment and the wrecking ball hanging over the long barracks. One glance was enough.

Sheriff Tobin met Adina at the doors to the long barracks, holding an injunction against her filed by the DRT who accused her of illegally taking over the premises.

"Miss Adina be reasonable," the sheriff begged, trying to hand her the papers. "You can't go in there. The ladies of the DRT have gotten this court order."

With a swift motion, Adina knocked the papers out of his hand and sent them flying. "I am a lady of the DRT," she roared, "and I will go in there and protect this building." Opening the door, she stepped inside to join the watchmen she'd posted on site and blocked the door.

The sheriff was powerless to stop Adina. He could threaten her not to enter the building, but once she was inside could not evict her without a further court order.

South wall of the old courtyard, looking northeast. Library of Congress, Historic American Building Survey, April 1938. Arthur W. Stewart, photographer.

The DRT was, of course, soon alerted to Adina's presence in the long barracks and they sent a member of what had become known as the Driscoll faction to the Alamo to find out exactly what was going on. Emma Kyle Burleson reported of the scene that several people including Mr. Hugo and Sheriff Tobin had gone to the door of the long barracks where Adina had barricaded herself to demand entry.

Tobin evidently told Adina's watchmen that he would break down the door with an axe. Receiving no answer, the sheriff took the axe to the door. When the party entered, they found Adina hiding behind some sort of desk or railing. The sheriff read the injunction to her, but, according to Burleson, Adina put her fingers in her ears and refused to either listen or leave the property. Her hired watchmen were evicted on threat of arrest and the rest of the group left, leaving behind the sheriff and a deputy who stepped outside briefly to confer and leaving Adina—who as a woman was a puzzle for the men to deal with—alone.

Left alone, in that moment, Adina moved quickly to the inner rooms of the building. She made her way, brushing cobwebs aside as she went, to the room where she believed Bowie had died and slammed and bolted that door from the inside. Then, feeling her way by the damp walls, she went to the window and opened the shutters. There she was reassured that the heavy iron grate would prevent anyone from getting into the room, and yet the window would allow her some light.

Adina was alone inside the structure she had fought to preserve. Looking out through the small opening, she saw that the crowd outside was increasing.

As the onlookers gathered around the sheriff, he said, "I'll force her out. Do not give her food or water. If you do, I'll arrest you. She'll come out soon enough."

He then set deputies to see that his orders were carried out.

Several of Clara Driscoll's supporters had arrived and stood in angry posture, arms crossed in front of them. One loudly demanded that the sheriff do something.

"Just like Santa Anna, show no leniency!" she shouted.

Adina would later say that she thought the woman was not behaving in a ladylike manner.

Almost ever since Clara Driscoll had written her first $5,000 check to Hugo and Schmeltzer in 1903, controversy had raged around the plans for preservation of the Alamo site and who would control the property.

When the state had reimbursed part of Clara Driscoll's investment in the long barracks in 1905, they had turned the custodianship of the entire property, including the chapel and the old convent building, over to the DRT. The initial agreement between the state and the DRT was that the De Zavala chapter, being the local chapter of the organization in San Antonio, would have control of the Alamo property—an agreement that was reached in part due to recognition of Adina's efforts to save the landmark. But in 1906, the DRT executive committee did an about-face and gave custodianship to Clara Driscoll, in recognition of her financial contribution. No records indicate whether or not Clara asked for this recognition, but she was on the executive committee of the DRT and De Zavala was not. Since she was in New York at the time, Clara arranged to have her longtime friend Florence Eager accept the keys to the structures and take temporary custodianship.

The heart of the dispute was shrouded in misunderstanding. Most people, regardless of their devotion to the memory of the defenders of the Alamo and their belief in the battle's importance in history, didn't know the real story of the brave men who defended the old mission from inside the long barracks. The attractive façade of the chapel made a more convenient and picturesque rallying point for the preservationists who wanted to honor the sacrifice of those men. It's unlikely that the focus on the chapel building was a willful misinterpretation of history. The true story of the battle was simply unknown by most people. Adina De Zavala knew the truth—which was why her aim had always been to preserve the long barracks. Clara Driscoll had, early on, responded to the myth and preferred to tear down that building in favor of creating a peaceful garden of remembrance around the chapel. A rift between the De Zavala faction and the Driscoll faction had opened up.

In April 1906, the DRT held its annual statewide convention in Goliad, a site perhaps chosen to commemorate the lives of the Texian heroes who died in the massacre there. By then the organization was divided into two camps as fiercely divided as the Texian Army and Santa Anna's troops, and the numbers were about as overwhelming in favor of Clara Driscoll. Adina's small but determined band of supporters was greatly outnumbered by the women who followed Clara. The rift over control of the Alamo had deepened, not healed, and at Goliad, it erupted.

Back in New York City, Clara Driscoll was puzzled and not a little bit offended by Adina's anger over the desire of some to demolish the long barracks. Clara was used to having people do as she wished, whether due to her charm or her money. She heard of Adina's vocal opposition from San Antonio supporters, but she didn't understand it. After all, Adina had sought her help, and in Clara's mind they were partners in the effort to save the Alamo. She was convinced that Adina would come around to her point of view and realize that the chapel must stand alone, surrounded by a beautiful park—a monument for the entire world to recognize and revere.

Clara was traveling from New York to Goliad that spring specifically to attend the convention, but her train had been delayed, and she would be late in arriving. In Goliad, Governor Samuel Lanham, who had once refused to appropriate funds for the Alamo, welcomed the ladies to the conference as a keynote speaker. Acutely aware of the conflict that was brewing—a conflict in which he himself was not an innocent bystander— he urged the women to have a pleasant meeting. "Put personal wishes and desires aside," he cautioned, "as you work toward your common goal of glorifying the history of this great state."

The women applauded his speech heartily.

The De Zavala chapter, the largest chapter of the DRT, seemed in control of the meeting from the beginning, despite their small numbers compared to the overall membership. In fact, one of the De Zavala Daughters was the chair of the conference, although a follower of Clara served as parliamentarian. The issue of custodianship of the Alamo surfaced almost immediately. One of Adina's supporters rose and was quickly recognized by the chair, who chose to ignore the parliamentarian if a point of order was brought up and to declare the member who brought it up out of order. In that manner, Adina's followers were able to pass motions they favored, including calling for elections from the floor rather than the executive committee. The executive committee, however, nullified the motion, claiming that their actions violated state laws governing incorporated associations.

The most contentious motion, of course, was about the custody of the Alamo site. When a member stood up and said, "I move that we return control of the mission to the De Zavala chapter and Adina De Zavala, effective November 11, 1906."[11] The women in the hall broke into a mixture of applause and objections.

"I move to amend the motion," one of Clara's supporters spoke up.

"The chair has not recognized you," was the response from the podium.

"Madame Chairman, I respectfully request permission to speak," said the determined woman.

The chair finally nodded, and the woman went on. "I move that we substitute Clara Driscoll Sevier's name for that of Adina De Zavala. Mrs. Sevier, known to most of us as our beloved Clara, provided the funds to purchase the long barracks and prevent a crass commercial hotel from being built on the spot."

Angry voices filled the small auditorium where they met. Some women even stamped their well-clad feet to express their dismay. The chairman banged her gavel on the podium repeatedly, shouting, "Ladies, ladies. Call for order." The squabbling continued, with women angrily facing each other and shouting. Adina De Zavala watched the scene with quiet amusement.

At long last, the noise died down. For once, the chairman recognized the parliamentarian for a closed vote. The parliamentarian replied, and the chairman announced, "Ladies, this is too delicate a matter, with passions running high. I cannot sanction a voice vote. Therefore, I have instructed our two marshals to distribute paper to each of you. Simply write the name of the person you wish to include in the motion. We will dismiss now and reconvene in thirty minutes."

This time the small room was filled with chatter, but the level of anger seemed to have died down. Members earnestly talked to each other, trying to persuade each in favor of their favorite. Clara Driscoll supporters kept watching the door to the room. They were convinced Clara's presence would give weight to their side. But she did not appear.

Thirty minutes later, to the second, the call came for order, ballots were collected, and other business was dealt with while the ballots were counted. During those thirty minutes, Clara Driscoll Sevier quietly snuck into the room and took a seat in the rear, unnoticed by the preoccupied women. The vote ultimately went to the De Zavala chapter—and Adina De Zavala.

The announcement was once again greeted with a mixture of applause and objections. Some ladies were so unladylike as to boo. Clara quieted the crowd by walking to the podium. She whispered in the chair's ear and then spoke.

"Above all, I wish for harmony with my sisters in this organization. Therefore, I hereby offer my resignation."

Real pandemonium broke out at that point. One report was that women yelled and screamed, and a newspaper cartoon depicted women dueling with rolling pins and umbrellas. It was Adina's turn to quiet the crowd. She, too, took to the podium, barely glancing at the woman who had once been her savior and was now her enemy in battle.

Speaking slowly and distinctly, Adina said, "I move that Mrs. Sevier be put in charge until November 11."

With complete self-control that revealed none of her tumultuous inner thoughts, Clara replied, "I decline the generous offer of Miss De Zavala."

Adina was quick with her response, carefully calculated to calm the crowd but not give up ground. "I therefore move that to compliment Mrs. Sevier and all she has done to save the Alamo, the convention honor the young lady she has asked to be custodian in her place, Miss Florence Eager."

Eager accepted the temporary post, and seemingly mollified, Clara then proposed the purchase of a portrait of Davy Crockett for the purpose of hanging it in the chapel. Her proposal was defeated. The group had decided any funds should go to restoring the long barracks. It was a rare defeat for Clara.

Clara returned to New York after the meeting but planned to be back in Texas by December. Her followers immediately began planning an Alamo demonstration[12] and plotting for the return of the property to DRT control—effectively Clara Driscoll's control.

By November, all thoughts of charity had flown from Adina's mind. During the intervening months, the long barracks had continued to crumble, and she had taken custody of several important historical artifacts within the building in order to protect them. Promptly on November 11, the date she had specified for the nominal protection of Florence Eager to end, she wrote to Eager to inform her that the De Zavala chapter was ready to take over the custodianship of the Alamo property.

"Are you ready to deliver the keys?" she demanded.

During the period between the convention and the planned turnover, however, the Driscoll faction, which dominated the executive committee in sheer numbers, had made good use of the six-month delay. They had begun the necessary paperwork to create a second DRT chapter in San Antonio, to be called the Alamo Mission chapter, with the intention of becoming the chapter that would have custody of the Alamo, a move that could delay the transfer of custody.

Adina raged in anger when she learned of their efforts. "They can't do that," she said aloud more than once as control of the Alamo slipped away from her.

She consoled herself that such administrative matters move slowly, and she was right. Any new chapter could not legally force possession until 1910, but the delay had given the Driscoll faction time to regroup and strategize in other ways, as well.

By the 1907 DRT convention, the split between the two bitterly opposed factions had not healed. That year the convention was held in

Austin, and pandemonium followed a morning of bickering over everything from who would conduct the meeting to early adjournment. Several senators and reporters—all male, of course—were present as observers. There was such contention over who would conduct the meeting that the woman presiding, a Driscollite, announced adjournment *sine die*. The Driscollites voted in favor of this adjournment for an indefinite time; the De Zavala group and most of the senators issued a loud voice vote opposing the announcement. The meeting adjourned, and the Driscollites stomped out of the Senate Chambers. Clara's followers would later claim that Adina's supporters had caused the commotion that led to the early adjournment. The De Zavala chapter claimed that the Driscoll women had made the meeting invalid by leaving.

Adina's followers stayed, elected their own officers to replace those who had left, and conducted a meeting. The Driscoll faction met later in the day and turned matters over to the executive committee, which voted to follow Clara's wishes and create a park, with grass and "trailing vines" around the Alamo. The DRT executive committee further told the governor that they wanted to buy back the long barracks from the state. Their intention was to wrest custody from the De Zavala chapter and demolish it.

The matter ended up in court when the Driscollites sought a temporary injunction to force the De Zavala group to relinquish custodianship of the Alamo and required that Adina give up the keys to the building and return the relics to the site. The case dragged on interminably. Adina suffered from the prolonged tension, at one point writing her lawyer, John T. Duncan, that she was on the "eve of nervous prostration." He replied with a letter encouraging her not to give up hope, but eventually the injunction was granted, and Adina had seemingly lost her battle.

When the word came, Adina clutched the keys to the long barracks in her hand as she hurried across Alamo Plaza, almost as driven as she had been the day she sought out Clara Driscoll. She tossed her head and her blue eyes flashed with anger. Even her posture as she strode along bespoke anger as she approached the watchman who was on duty.

"Miss Adina, you can't go in there. You know that. Things have changed." The watchman spoke tentatively, still afraid of offending the woman who had been in charge for a long time.

"Things are going to change even more," she said, anger making her voice harsh and strong. "I'm not through fighting to save the Alamo."

"Miss Adina, give me the keys, and I'll see that they go to the proper person," the watchman replied.

"You are looking at the proper person," Adina stormed as she unlocked the door and started into the gloomy interior. Then she whirled and faced the watchman, as though he represented all the forces aligned against her.

"Did you know," she stormed, "that the DRT has filed a lawsuit against me, claiming that I have stolen relics from the mission and must return them?" She stamped her foot in anger. "I took some things that I thought were not secure here. They are safely at my home. I will return them when I am assured they will be under lock and key." Then she really did disappear into the gloom.

It would be Adina's first occupation of the Alamo.

The court case, begun in 1907, finally went to trial and was decided in favor of Clara Driscoll's group, the Alamo chapter. They were declared the official DRT group in charge of the Alamo grounds. Clara Driscoll began to solicit funds from friends for the demolition of the long barracks and creation of a beautiful park. Adina countered this campaign with plats, maps, and other evidence to support her claim about the significance of the Hugo and Schmeltzer building. Her documents also showed that the chapel was in ruins at the time of the battle, and that the defenders could not possibly have held off the Mexican Army from inside its walls. They needed the fortification the long barracks provided. Adina bombarded the governor's office with her documentation.

Her research included a statement from Adele Briscoe Looscan, a DRT founder and its historian, who protested the ignorance of those who claimed the chapel was the site of the massacre, and statements from an U.S. army captain and a Mexican soldier that the barracks was the bloodiest spot. John Henry Brown, a respected Texas historian, in his *Brown's History of Texas*, quoted an officer who had visited Bowie on his sick bed in the barracks.

Adina's biggest coup, though, came when she located Don Enrique Esparza, a man of seventy whose father had died at the Alamo. After the battle, he and his mother and three siblings walked out of the chapel. (Previously, it had been believed that Mrs. Dickinson and her daughter were the only survivors.) Although he was a young child at the time, Esparza retained a detailed memory of the mission and added a great deal to the history of the battle, according to De Zavala.

Years later, Adina recalled that during this time her telephone was tapped and historical matter she sent to the governor disappeared either at the San Antonio or the Austin post office. Calling it an irretrievable loss of historical documents, she said she once heard a man was arrested for taking mail from the post office and served a prison sentence.

Adina's opponents had little but a conviction that the chapel made a more picturesque symbol of the martyrdom. In truth, the crumbling and roofless chapel was indefensible; the long barracks had been fortified and provided enough shelter that the Texians slaughtered an astounding number of Mexican soldiers before their defeat.

After the DRT won custody of the site, the De Zavala chapter learned that the DRT had arranged to lease the barracks but only until the structure could be torn down. Clara Driscoll offered to pay for the demolition. "We will put a park around the chapel, no distracting buildings, and it will stand in all its solitary glory," she decreed. "The barracks was not part of the original mission." Ignoring the historical record, Clara claimed that the army had built the structure when it used the mission as an ordnance warehouse.[13] She was apparently interested in beauty, not historical accuracy. To this day, no one knows if Clara truly believed the fighting took place in the chapel or not.

When Adina learned from colleagues on the DRT executive committee that the wrecking ball was poised to destroy the long barracks she fumed, "I should have stopped this a few years back when we had that blasted cup of tea. I could tell she didn't know her history and was only concerned with the appearance of history. I knew her help would come at a high price."

However, Adina had developed a plan for just such a contingency and had even written her lawyer about it, though he refused to sanction her scheme for fear of being cited for contempt of court. In February 1908, she knew that the time for action had come—the wrecking ball was paid for, thanks to Clara, and ready to swing.

Adina's plan was ruthless. Taking pen in hand, she wrote a letter to the acting DRT president, a Mrs. Wharton Bates, authorizing her to turn the Alamo keys over to Adina De Zavala. Adina signed the letter, "Mary Briscoe, secretary general." Madams Bates and Briscoe were verified officers of the DRT—but they were also part of the De Zavala faction—and Adina felt confident of their support of her scheme.

Adina then went to Charles Heuermann, a longtime employ of Hugo and Schmeltzer who had physical custody of the disputed Alamo keys but who had given them to her many times before. Innocent of the intrigue afoot and the division within the DRT, he thought nothing of giving Miss De Zavala the keys. Adina then hired three watchmen and installed them in the long barracks, replacing the DRT locks with her own.

Then, on that cold and dreary morning, Adina stormed the gates.

Inside, having defied the sheriff, Adina took stock of her small quarters in the light from the barred window. A couple of empty cases labeled "Whisky" were piled along one wall, and there was an empty paint can in the room that she could use as a privy. A pile of burlap bags sat in one corner. Apparently, the bags had once held cement for they were covered with a powdery white dust.

Adina felt very small and very alone. But she would not give in. As the day wore on, she grew desperately thirsty and felt the first pangs of hunger. Toward evening, when the crowd had drifted away, the sheriff—in defiance of his own order—slipped her a canteen of cool water. She sipped gratefully, restraining her thirst so that the water would last all night.

To sleep, Adina piled the burlaps bags together to make a mat on the floor, but they didn't make a comfortable bed. She could hear rodents scurrying around the room and lay in terror that they would climb over her. Doubts crept into her mind—was she making a foolish, futile gesture? Did anyone else care about the long barracks? The world outside was dark and still, and loneliness came over her again.

If she slept, it was fitfully, dreaming that she was visited by the ghosts of Travis and Crockett and Bonham. When dawn came, she rose stiffly from her uncomfortable bed, made a modest toilette before opening the shutters, and tried her best to re-pin what had the day before been her bouffant hairdo. If she had had a mirror, she'd have seen that her face was streaked with dirt, and powdery white dust clung to her hair. She dared not waste the precious bit of water in the canteen for washing.

In the morning, the sheriff, less gruff than the front he put on, turned his head when a fellow member of the De Zavala chapter poured coffee through a pipe and slipped one end of the pipe through the window. Two other supporters smuggled food to Adina. One used a pulley system to get a bag of sandwiches to her when she stood on an upper galley; another supposedly passed chocolates to her in full view of the sheriff's men by hiding the sweets in newspapers.

As the morning wore on, the crowd regathered outside, and a fiesta-like atmosphere developed. Mariachis played, some of the chili queens brought their stands to the Alamo Plaza, and shabby women went through the crowd selling trinkets. The *San Antonio Light* headline on February 11, 1908, read, "Miss Adina De Zavala Enacts Siege of the Alamo all over again and Defies Deputy Sheriff."

Adina's adventure made headlines across the country. The nation was captivated by a lone woman brave enough to fly in the face of the law—and of her fellow members of the DRT—and, alone, occupy a crumbling old building. Reporters played up her belief that the actual battle took place in the long barracks, not the chapel, and she won the nation's sympathy for her determination to preserve the truth. The story was picked up by the *New York Times*, the *Washington Post*, the *Los Angeles Times*, and the *Atlanta Constitution*. Across the country, Americans applauded Adina's fortitude, as they had previously lauded Clara's remarkable generosity.

Inside her fortress, however, Adina felt trapped, like an animal in a cage that people had come to taunt or a criminal on display. After all, she thought, she was a criminal, wasn't she? She was inside the building in defiance of a court order. And when she did emerge—for she knew she would have to sometime—the sheriff might arrest her. As the hours dragged on, she paced, and most of all, she avoided going near enough to the grated window so that the crowd could see her. The one time she did, a great shout arose. She detected cheers, but she also heard some scurrilous comments.

Her thoughts wandered back to Travis and his men. Had the trapped sensation she felt overcome them? Did they have second thoughts? Regrets? They of course knew their destiny, and it was much grimmer than whatever awaited her. But briefly, she felt a strong kinship with her heroes.

After she emerged from the building, contradictory stories about her vigil flew across the country. Newspapers played up the hardships she had endured—no food, no lights, coffee snuck to her through a tube, and a grate over her window. Deputies on duty at the Alamo said she had food, water, lights, electricity, and use of a telephone. But the other version of the story was more dramatic.

During her time barricaded in that one room, Adina continually insisted she would only turn the keys over to the government—not to Clara Driscoll or the DRT. On the third day of her siege, she negotiated an agreement, through her grated window, to give control of the Alamo back to the state superintendent of public buildings, though she would have much preferred to keep it with the De Zavala chapter. The DRT, fully aware of the bad publicity they had received from the incident, agreed to the negotiated settlement, though the papers they had filed for the injunction clearly indicated that they still wanted to tear down the long barracks and replace it with a park or a museum.

Adina's escapade got the attention of the governor and the Texas legislature, all of whom had previously dismissed the disagreement as a ladies' quarrel over tea. They now took it seriously.

In the days following her occupation, Adina De Zavala issued a public statement in which she echoed the wording of Colonel Travis's famous "Victory or Death" letter. "Where he wrote, 'I shall never retreat or surrender,'" she boasted, "I did not surrender nor retreat." Indeed, she had won the major battle—the long barracks of the Alamo was preserved.

"I had heard," she later said, "that possession was nine points of the law. There was nothing else for me to do but hold the fort, and so I did."

Her long hours of solitude were probably the high point of her life.

The DRT responded by announcing it would no longer recognize Adina nor the twelve members of her De Zavala chapter as members of the DRT. The group held to their firm belief in the unimportance of the long-barracks building and their plans to create a garden of remembrance and museum in its place. They steadfastly claimed that the entire episode was unnecessary, since the Hugo and Schmeltzer building had nothing to do with the Alamo and was built long after the fall of the

Alamo.[14] The DRT went so far as to suggest that Adina had barricaded herself simply as a publicity stunt. The rest of her long life, Adina never forgave nor forgot. She was a vocal and frequent critic of the DRT and what she saw as their casual, even slipshod, approach to historical detail and accuracy.

Members of the original De Zavala's Daughters remained loyal to Adina and her cause, as did Adele Briscoe Looscan of Houston, the DRT's historian, who withdrew from the organization in support of Adina. Both she and Adina were courted by the new Texas State Historical Association and became longtime members. At one point in the 1930s, Mrs. Looscan would serve as president of that organization.

After Adina's occupation of the long barracks, the legislature opted to postpone any decision about the property until after elections, which brought a new governor, Oscar B. Colquitt. The governor toured the Alamo, met with both Adina and Clara, and after three months took control of the property from the DRT on the grounds that it had done nothing to improve the site in six years. The DRT again went to court, and an appeals court ruled against the governor, who took the matter to the Texas Supreme Court, which reaffirmed the judgment of the lower court and overturned that of the court of appeals decision which had given control to the Alamo chapter of the DRT. The state could make improvements on the Alamo, but again it was the subject of long, drawn-out, and probably expensive court cases. Passions about the Alamo still ran high.

Meanwhile, there was Alamo action of another kind in the works.

The specter of a hotel to be built overlooking the site still loomed. One Charles Reeves of St. Louis notified Adina that a hotel company had purchased property directly behind the long barracks and announced their support of the plan to raze the unsightly building, making a park of the area to highlight what he called the "historic blood-stained chapel." Their letter to Adina implied that the DRT and the state both supported the plan. Adina wrote back politely, explaining the significance of the building and her plan for turning it into a museum. The businessman who had written her was scornful of her idea and threatened to cancel the hotel project, which would have been fine with Adina. But the DRT board, confident of the governor's support, agreed to negotiate with the hotel firm, and a newspaper article all but gave Clara credit for it. Since she was now nationally recognized as the Savior of the Alamo, her wishes for the site were considered written in stone. Architect Harvey Page reappeared, with landscaping plans for the park that would replace the long barracks.

The governor, however, firmly told the DRT that while it had full permission to improve the property, it was not sanctioned to order the destruction.

In 1911, Governor Oscar B. Colquitt called a special meeting in San Antonio to consider the future of the Alamo. He invited the De Zavala supporters and the Driscoll followers, and he made it clear that he would listen to both sides but would align with neither. At the meeting, the Driscoll group maintained their claim that the walls of the long barracks were of no consequence. They believed that the wooden grocery store structure was not a mere superstructure under which the masonry walls of the original convent could still be found. The governor, wanting to preserve history and hoping that facts would support him, declared that the wooden superstructure should come down, but that the original two-story masonry walls should remain. When those original walls were revealed, it became clear that they were in disrepair and partially gone with time and looting, but the governor declared they would be restored to their original state at the time of the battle. However, the restoration work was not immediately completed due to a lack of funding, and in 1913, while Governor Colquitt was out of the state, his lieutenant governor had the upper story torn down. The Driscoll side had won a small, symbolic victory. It was, wrote mission historian Frank Thompson, a victory of image over history.

The DRT annual meetings in 1906, 1907, and 1908 had given custody of the Alamo to the De Zavala group. But Driscoll's followers had
always found a way to circumvent these decisions. Adina was fighting
a battle not only against Clara's beautification dream but also against
area businessmen. The Alamo sat on valuable real estate property. Many
men thought control of the mission should be taken from the quarrelling
women. A 1909 court decision finalized the Alamo chapter's control of
the property and satisfied Clara's earlier request for "a little return for
my work." The case for control of the site was not finally settled until
1913.

Adina De Zavala never gave up trying to gain official recognition
of the significance of the long barracks. In 1936 she traveled to Dallas,
ostensibly for the Texas Centennial Celebration but in reality to gain
support in her battle with the Alamo chapter. And a drawn-out battle it
was. She filed a complaint with the state about misleading signs in the
chapel, erroneously marking the significant locations such as Crockett's
death spot or the place where Susanna Dickinson hid with her daughter Angelina. Visitors never saw the real site of the battle, she protested,
unless they knew the true story and sought out the long barracks.

The Alamo was her first significant project, and she felt she had
failed. Yet, she didn't. Because of her, the long barracks today houses a
museum and sees many visitors.

CHAPTER SEVEN

———•◦•———

Adina and the Ongoing Battle

In 1907, in the midst of her fight over the long barracks, Adina retired from teaching, in part, one suspects, because of a parental accusation of cruel and unjust treatment of a student. Adina's refusal to compromise her beliefs carried through to her teaching life, and she refused to placate the complaining parent. In truth, Adina likely did not have the patient character a teacher needed. Teaching had turned out not to be her life's work. Giving it up was a turning point in her life. Apparently, there was enough money in the family that Adina did not need to produce an income and could devote herself to preservation. It was her self-appointed cause, the mission for which she felt she was destined, and she was so obsessed by her cause that she had neither time nor energy for other interests. She lived in a house near downtown San Antonio with her mother and sister. She had few friends, only read what helped her historical studies, apparently was not a housekeeper or a cook.

Adina De Zavala didn't particularly care what people thought of her. She was quick of mind and quick of tongue, although her sense of humor often provided a saving grace. She knew some people considered her difficult, a nuisance, a pest—none of that mattered in the face of what she felt she was called upon to accomplish. She admired Davy Crockett, one of the Alamo heroes, who is purported to have said, "Make sure you're

Adina De Zavala in front of the fireplace at her home, 141 Taylor Street in San Antonio. The house no longer stands, and the address appears to be the back door of a Baptist church. San Antonio Light / San Antonio Express-News / ZUMA Press.

right. Then go ahead." At best, she could be called intellectually curious, perhaps even eccentric; some critics saw her as combative. Adina never doubted that she was right—about anything.

Well before the second battle, in 1887, De Zavala had founded the Daughters and Sons of the Heroes and Pioneers of the Republic of Texas, along with its more public counterpart, the Texas Historical and Landmark Association, a statewide organization of men and women that placed historical markers at various sites. In 1912, when the DRT refused to recognize the membership of the original De Zavala Daughters, the members of the chapter joined ranks with the Texas Historical and Landmark Association. Eventually, there were chapters of the association in several cities and towns in addition to San Antonio. The association was active until the early 1950s. With eight members, the De Zavala Daughters met annually for business and a program of history. The last recorded reference to the group was in 1953.

The first marker placed by the group was at the grave of Ben Milam, who had died in 1835 leading Texian volunteers against the Mexican troops. A statue and monument to Milam were later placed at the site, and a commemorative flag has flown there ever since. Annually on the anniversary of the fall of the Alamo, known as "Texas Heroes Day," a ceremony is held there honoring all Texas heroes. That day was a favorite celebration for Adina. The association would go on to place twenty-eight markers in the city of San Antonio and ten outside it.

Adina also championed the cause of naming local public schools after significant people in Texas history. The group eagerly took up the task and submitted a list of names for the previously numbered schools, all of which were accepted and all of which came straight from the pages of Texas history. They also worked to preserve historic street names, opposing Anglicization of the names.

Adina was concerned with not only the Alamo but also with the five other area missions that have been described as the roots of San Antonio history. Eventually, with the preservation of the missions around San Antonio secured, her interest branched out to missions in East Texas, and she extended her vision into western Louisiana.

Adina didn't believe in limiting her research to documents and maps. She wanted to experience the past firsthand, and that meant searching out sites now abandoned and overgrown.

In 1935 she and her friend Frances Donecker traveled extensively throughout East Texas. Although she was slight and somewhat frail looking, Adina was tougher than she appeared. When on the trail of a site, she paid no attention to discomforts and willingly pushed through brush and swamps, looking for precise locations of historic structures. Sometimes she did physical work, such as roof repair or moving stones and woodwork. Donecker, a teacher, was apparently less hardy than Adina but she was more organized, and usually went with her. Whereas Adina's notes were disorganized and could rarely be deciphered by anyone but herself, Donecker took careful and detailed notes and organized them precisely, preserving the record of their efforts just as Adina fought to preserve the sites themselves.

Once, as they tramped through brush in the Piney Woods in 1935, Donecker looked down and saw her gown covered in red spots—sand ticks. Too frightened to move, she stood as if paralyzed until another woman with the party brushed them off. Adina paid no attention to the bugs and pushed on, but according to Donecker's records, she was badly bitten and "suffered the tortures of the damned for several days." Adina was then seventy-four years old.

On one trip, when she was forced to stay overnight in a small town, the local residents were curious about her. Adina later told the story of her encounters to an interviewer.[15]

"What's your business?" a man asked.

She shrugged, "No business. I came from San Antonio to look for some historical sites and try to save the Stone Fort."

The man looked skeptical. "You must be selling something," he persisted.

The scene was repeated several times with various natives of the area, and Adina later reported that she rarely had such fun.

Frances Donecker was apparently known through East Texas for her historical work and had developed many friendships. Due to her connections, the two women were invited into people's homes, fed well, and schooled on local sites of historical interest. The women attended dedication ceremonies for the state park at the Mission San Francisco de los Tejas, drove up and down rough roads, ferried across the Sabine River, visited a veneering mill and toured a plantation, soaked up endless tales of local history, and were front-page news in several small-town weekly newspapers.

Adina's sly humor comes out in her record of this trip. "Miss D. is trying to convert me from drinking coffee, but I believe she has a hopeless task before her." And of herself, she wrote, "Me—on the surface, a calm, prosaic, phlegmatic veteran school marm. Inside a repressed sentimental enthusiastic sentimentalist." One night they took the only room they could get in a small town. It had a single bed and a cot, and Adina wrote that both looked none too clean. In her journal, she recorded, "What a night, sleeping on a ladder, a highway in the front yard, a railroad in the back yard, and worst of all, a suspicion of the presence of unwelcome bed-fellows."

Although she never found the Old Stone Fort, she did locate the approximate site of two early missions—San Francisco de los Tejas and Santíssimo Nombre de María. The sites were designated with granite and bronze markers. The former was thought to be the first permanent white settlement in Texas. Thanks to Adina, the site has a state park, a replica of the original log mission building, and a historic marker.

Except for an occasional foray into Louisiana, Adina's interests did not range beyond the borders of her native state. If she ever longed to see the wonders of Europe that had so impressed Clara, she never admitted to it. Her only verified trip outside the United States was to Mexico City for research. One might suspect some hostility toward her on the part of Mexico, since her grandfather was, in their eyes, a deserter. But she reported she was treated well and given a private tour of a major museum.

"Would you like to see Maximilian's carriage?" the museum functionary asked.

Adina wanted to see anything of historical importance, and she knew well the history of the ruler who had been the only monarch of the Second Mexican Empire, having upset the democratic government of the Mexican Republic. Maximilian invaded the Mexican Republic and defeated President Benito Juárez in 1861. He declared himself emperor in 1864. When the United States emerged from its own Civil War, it turned part of its attention to Mexico and sent direct aid to forces led by Benito Juárez. Maximilian's empire collapsed, and he was captured and executed by the Mexican government. The Republic was restored.

All this history went through Adina's mind, but she simply smiled at the man, took the arm he offered, and said, "Of course."

"This is," her guide said, "much grander than the plain black carriage in which the emperor was driven to his execution."

They stood before an ornate gold carriage with red side panels and red curtains. When the functionary let down the steps, she saw that the entire carriage was lined with white silk.

"Would you like to sit inside?" he asked.

Surprised, she could only nod. She mounted the steps, settled herself on one of the plush seats, and looked out the window. For just a moment, she felt like an empress, but royalty, especially royalty that had usurped a legitimate government, did not appeal to her. She had inherited her grandfather's rigorous devotion to democratic principles. She quickly scrambled out of the carriage. Texas missions were more to her taste.

After the Alamo, Adina's most important preservation project was the Spanish Governor's Palace in San Antonio. An adobe structure first planned in 1722 and completed in 1749, the so-called palace sits in the middle of the bustling city. It was built for the captain of the presidio, the fort meant to protect the missions, inhabited by the representative of the king of Spain. When the presidio closed, the palace was occupied by the governor named by the royal government. The building is unique because of the coat of arms over its door, which initially attracted Adina's attention, and because it is the only ancient municipal building of its kind in America.

As San Antonio's population grew, the palace's location worked against it. It was adjacent to the Military Plaza, which had been home to the city's famed chili queens for more than a hundred years. The "queens" and their chaperones arrived at twilight and set out their pots. The young women who served the chili wore Spanish costumes and mantillas, spread checkered cloths on long tables, lit their booths with oil lamps, and flirted outrageously with customers—usually under the

Patio, Spanish Governor's Palace. Library of Congress.

watchful eye of Mama or Papa. They sold chili, frijoles, and enchiladas. Until dawn, the plaza was alive with people—tourists, soldiers, serenading troubadours—and it was noisy. There were no class distinctions—a man about town, seeking a late snack after an evening of dancing, food, and tequila, might find himself seated at a long table next to a boot black. Both enjoyed the food—and even more so, the company of the young women. The last occupants of the palace, a family named Perez, left because of the noise and confusion.

The Governor's Palace was rented to small businesses, rather like stalls in an arcade. At any given time, there might have been a used-clothing store, an antique store offering goods of questionable provenance, even a bar and café.

By 1915, when Adina first became interested in the once-palatial residence, it was an eyesore. The keystone, that wedge-shaped piece of stone at the top of the arched doorway that holds all other stones in place, bore the coat of arms of the royal family of Hapsburg and the inscription "Se acabo 1749"—finished in 1749. For Adina, that was proof that this

Well in the courtyard of the Governor's Palace in San Antonio. Library of Congress.

dilapidated building was the original governor's palace. Its architecture was typical of the homes of grandees or noblemen in Spain.

She began her research, finding lots of dead ends but an occasional reference from a surprising source, such as the note in explorer Zebulon Pike's journal that he had visited San Antonio and been escorted through the Spanish Governor's Palace, probably in the first decade of the nineteenth century. A couple of wills in old Spanish families gave her the original layout of the building and an idea of some of the fine china and jewels it held. She even found an old painting showing a feast in the "long room." Simultaneous with her research, Adina began efforts to save the building, following at first much the same pattern she had established with the Alamo. She took an option on the property before she had any money in hand with which to purchase it.

She appealed to the city for funding to restore the building, with no results. She and her supporters practically begged on the streets. But then someone paid attention—a member of the newly established San Antonio Conservation Society, Mrs. Elizabeth Graham. Her mother had supported Adina during her three-day siege of the Alamo. Mrs. Graham, who became the second curator of the Governor's Palace, recounted that one city politician advised the city to put something in their bond issue that would appeal to the ladies. The restoration of the palace was included, the bond issue passed, and the Spanish Governor's Palace was restored and rededicated.

Another unfortunate parallel to Adina's Alamo experience cropped up. The Conservation Society had pushed to have another item included in the bond issue, and they took credit for the bond issue, crowding Adina out. But she had learned her lesson, and this time she protested loud and long, claiming that the society was encroaching on her field of operations.

"There's just no room for anyone else," she wrote, "so clear out."

The interior staircase at the Governor's Palace in San Antonio. When Adina De Zavala worked to save it, it was one story, but she was convinced it was originally two—partly because of this staircase, which now goes to nothing but a closet. Library of Congress.

Two members of the society met with Adina and claimed to have worked things out, but the society never recognized Adina's role in saving the palace. Elizabeth Graham, however, publicly testified to Adina's central role, saying the society "helped," but the major effort came from Miss De Zavala. She saved the palace; the Conservation Society got the credit.

And once again there was a second-story debate. And once again, Adina's instincts about historical sites proved accurate, in spite of court documents that described the building as having one story. At the time Adina worked to restore it, the palace clearly had only one story. But there was an obvious clue that it might once have had at least a partial second story: a graceful curving staircase led to nothing more than a tiny room used for storage.

Adina wanted to restore the building to its original state and then use it as a museum, perhaps to house some of her growing collection of artifacts. Again, she lost this portion of the battle. Adina's dreams of glorious history were not always practical in her twentieth-century world.

In the 1930s, Adina wanted to move her family's graves at Zavala Point to a safer location near San Jacinto due to the prevalent flooding in the area. Lorenzo Jr., her eldest brother, objected to the move, saying he had promised their father the graves would never be disturbed, and Adina lost her bid to relocate the cemetery. However, she carefully recorded the plat of the graveyard, locating and documenting each grave, and when her fears were realized after Buffalo Bayou flooded the land in the 1960s, her preservation instincts were proved correct once again, even after her death. The documents she left were critical to the restoration. (Later, when the Houston Ship Channel was built, conservation groups lobbied for moving the graves. The headstones were moved, but the bodies and caskets were too badly deteriorated.)

The surviving De Zavala family also brought a lawsuit in an attempt to recover the original homestead land at Zavala Point. After Lorenzo's death, Emily remarried, and her new husband applied to be administrator of the estate, edging out Lorenzo Jr. To complicate the estate, Lorenzo Sr. had apparently adopted his second wife's son, Henry, from a previous relationship or marriage—no one is quite sure nor is there absolute certainty that Emily herself gave birth to the child. But Henry schemed for years to gain part of the inheritance and engaged Adina in lengthy correspondence. The inheritance rights were further complicated by a man calling himself Pedro de Zavala, who claimed to be the sole heir. After lengthy court battles, in which Adina was heavily involved, the courts decided against Adina, and she was left only with childhood memories of a rose garden she treasured as a child. She may well have seen this legal battle as another failure to preserve a part of the past.

Not only in field notes but in other aspects of her life, Adina was notoriously disorganized. Her study, a room sacred to her in the home she shared with her mother and sister, was a disaster of papers, notes, books. Once, when going on one of her exploratory trips, she posted a note on the door of her private apartment saying no one should enter

Adina sitting in the doorway of the Veramundi House (Spanish Governor's Palace). Adina
Emilia De Zavala Papers, The Dolph Briscoe Center for American History, The University of Texas at Austin.

during her absence without her written permission. "My historical notes are scattered everywhere—and it would set me back to be worried about them." In another instance, her sister, Mary, disposed of fifty-seven cartons of research. Though De Zavala bemoaned the loss, it made little dent in her output.

Adina's mother died in 1918; her sister Mary in 1950. Her other siblings had also died, and as the sole survivor of the family in her later years she had enough money to fund her research and even hire a part-time secretary. For a while, the secretary even lived in the De Zavala home, but she was unable to make much headway in organizing her employer's papers.

In spite of the disorder, Adina was a prolific writer, using the notes and research she had collected over the years as source for the many projects she had in her mind. The result was a monumental collection. Her three most important books deal with the Alamo: *Story of the Siege and Fall of the Alamo* (privately published, 1911); *History and Legends of the Alamo and Other Missions in and around San Antonio* (privately published, 1917; reprinted by Arte Publico Press, 1996); and *The Alamo: Where the Last Man Died* (published posthumously by the Naylor Company, 1956). This last book was financed by the Texas Historical and Landmark Association. De Zavala also wrote magazine and newspaper articles and pamphlets. Because of the scattered and ephemeral nature of her writings, a full and complete bibliography may never be achieved. Her interest in folklore is evident in the titles of some brief pieces of writing: "Texas History—Written and Unwritten," a 1905 piece in which she claimed that women wrote a goodly proportion of the state's history, "being quick to perceive the romance and the beauty of history"; "The Enchanted Rock—The Hill of the Original Woman in Blue"; "How the Huisache Received Its Bloom"; "Red Feather—The Origin of the Red Bird," about a king of Texas before the Spanish arrived. Other essays display the wide range of her interests: "Mothers Tensions in Home

Insurance," about the Widowed Mother's Pension, and "A Review of the Erection of the Alamo."

Some years before her death, Adina arranged to donate all her papers, documents, and relics to the University of Texas at Austin. Today they reside in the archives of the Barker Center for American History. The university sent a secretary to San Antonio to help Miss De Zavala organize her material for transfer to the archives. The secretary, Bess Fitzhugh, wrote in dismay at the mess she encountered. Miss Fitzhugh paid periodic visits to San Antonio during the last years of Adina's life but, writing in the 1990s, historian Gale Hamilton Shiffrin found the archive at the Barker still a wild mess.

Praised throughout her lifetime for her strength, in spite of her small stature and appearance of fragility, Adina De Zavala had a restless energy about her. Yet as she grew older, she suffered many of the problems of aging. At the age of eighty-three, she fell and broke her hip. She made only a partial recovery and toward the end of her life moved about her house by relying on the support of furniture. She had cataracts in both eyes, which progressively limited her vision and were apparently never corrected. She devised her own methods for coping, such as a way of folding one- and five-dollar bills so that she could tell them apart. She used no other currency. Although she continued to live alone, she had a secretary and household help, enabling her to manage. She was in and out of the hospital during her last years, but she continued to work. Once, visiting her, Frances Donecker found papers and Texana material strewn all over her hospital bed. A small Texas flag stood on the bedside table.

Well before her death, Adina left her estate, including some 350 books but excluding her archive, to the University of the Incarnate Word. She had also generously donated to the university over the years. In gratitude, the sisters regularly checked on her well-being. At one point, Adina was moved to the infirmary at the university for several weeks. She fell again and was transferred to Santa Rosa Hospital, where she went into a coma and died on March 1, 1955.

Her funeral was held on March 3, just days before the anniversary of the fall of the Alamo. The funeral procession, with the casket draped with a Texas flag, paused as it passed by the Alamo. She is buried in the family plot at St. Mary's Cemetery.

Adina was active in many historical and San Antonio organizations. She was a charter member and an honorary fellow of the Texas State Historical Association, a member of the San Antonio Conservation Society, the committee of one hundred to plan the Texas bicentennial celebration. She belonged to the United Daughters of the Confederacy, the Texas Women's Press Association, the Society of Arts and Letters, the Texas Philosophical Society, the Witte Museum Arts League, the Old Trail Drivers Association, and several others.

In spite of Adina's history of preservation and her active role in civic affairs, the DRT clung for over forty-five years to its identification of Clara Driscoll as the Savior of the Alamo. In plaques and pamphlets, no mention was made of Adina. Change did not begin until the late 1990s when Adina's picture was finally hung in one of the rooms of the small museum the DRT operated in the restored convent or long-barracks building. A ceramic plaque in the courtyard brought Adina and Clara together, at least on the surface, in acknowledging them as joint saviors of the Alamo. And a Wall of History in the courtyard, near the chapel, recognized Adina's part in the story.

The Texas Historical Commission was equally slow to recognize Miss De Zavala. A 1990 article in their quarterly publication, *The Medallion*, was titled "Who Really Saved the Alamo?" but made no mention of her, citing instead a group of other people who had assisted Clara. But in 1991, an article appeared titled "Adina De Zavala, Preservationist Extraordinaire."

Within a month of Adina's death, the Texas State Legislature passed a resolution citing her as a living symbol of the contributions of

Spanish-speaking patriots. The trouble with that is that she had grown up in an English-speaking household and was not fluent in Spanish. Three of her grandparents and her mother were Irish, and her father was only half Mexican. But in Texas in those days, a small bit of Mexican heritage—and a Mexican last name—identified you.

Although Adina was inordinately proud of the achievements of her Mexican grandfather, she did not identify herself as Mexican. In a rare reference to the subject, she once described herself as an American of Mexican descent. She referred to poor Mexicans as "them" not "us." But she was quick to see that preserving the Mexican part of the Texas story was as important as telling the Anglo story, and most of the historic sites she preserved—missions and the Governor's Palace—date back to Hispanic Texas.

The legislature directed the DRT to install a plaque at the Alamo in her honor, a direct request that was ignored for forty years. It was the late 1990s before the Texas Historic Marker in her honor was placed on the Plaza. Once the DRT recognized their responsibility, controversy over the location of the plaque apparently accounted for it languishing in the basement of the Bexar County Courthouse for a lengthy time. Some historians said it should be on the long barracks and not several hundred yards away. Others saw the delay as part of a Texas failure to recognize its central Mexican heritage—a stretch given Adina's thoughts on her mixed ancestry and her attitude about the Mexican people. Most historical markers are made of aluminum but this one is bronze to ensure its survival in the elements. The marker erroneously states that Adina barricaded herself inside the long barracks in 1907; the true date is 1908.

The earliest scholarly attention to Adina's preservation work was probably the 1967 article "The Second Battle of the Alamo," by Robert L. Ables. The article was apparently an outgrowth of his 1955 master's thesis presented to the Universities of Mexico City College.

In 1995, DRT member Lee Spencer formed a new organization, the Alamo Defenders Descendants Association, to honor those who fought for the Alamo. With membership limited to directed and lateral descendants of those who fought at the Alamo, the association strives to promote, preserve, and exchange historical data about the Alamo, perpetuate the memory of the defenders, aid in the preservation of the Alamo and related sites, and mark gravestones of the defendants. Members meet for an annual remembrance ceremony on Alamo Plaza. The group's website, alamodescendants.org, has alphabetical lists of defenders, scouts and couriers, and noncombatant survivors.

Recent scholars, such as Gale Hamilton Shiffrin, have researched Adina's accomplishments carefully and without bias. In their book, *Las Tejanas: 300 Years of History*, Teresa Palomo Acosta and Ruthe Winegarten call De Zavala the first to write Tejana history and claim she saw that histories were ignoring Spanish history. Because of her Anglo heritage and class privilege, she had access to education, but she was not particularly conscious of women's history. At least one scholar, Richard Flores, seems to have brought his own prejudice to a lengthy introduction to the 1996 reprint of *History and Legends of the Alamo and Other Missions in and around San Antonio*. Flores attacks the DRT for focusing on the battle and not the Alamo's history as a mission. Pointing out that only thirteen of the defenders were native Texans, he accuses the DRT of "racializing" the battle, making it a racial war in order to justify Anglo dominance in Texas culture. He claims the Alamo glorification is all about keeping Mexicans in their place. In her master's thesis, Suzanne Seifert Cottraux picks up on Flores's theme, claiming that Adina's motivation came less from her passion for history than from her desire to be part of "Texas Royalty"— rich Anglo Texans. Linking her to the Texas Women's Club Movement, Cottraux suggests that Adina, like many women, needed something to give meaning to her life, "a characteristic of women who are unsure of themselves." It's a theory that diminishes Adina's accomplishments.

Throughout her long life, Adina kept notes of her preservation work, her achievements and disappointments, and these notes are available to the public at the Barker Center for American History on the campus of the University of Texas and in the De Zavala Collection at San Antonio's University of the Incarnate Word.

Adina De Zavala probably wasn't familiar with Henry David Thoreau's theory of civil disobedience, but she employed the technique, if not the term, to save the Alamo. Her dedicated preservation work paved the way for the creation of San Antonio's famed River Walk and the restoration of La Villita, that square block of vintage shops, art galleries, and restaurants in the heart of downtown. When Adina first dedicated herself to saving the Alamo, the notion of historical accuracy was in its infancy. No one had defined "to preserve." It could as well have meant beauty, as it did to Clara, as historical accuracy, which was the interpretation to which Adina held throughout her life. She was a pioneer in establishing the concept of historical preservation as it is known today.

She was a passionate Texan, and as one scholar wrote of her feisty and stubborn personality, her own worst enemy. Her role in saving the Alamo has been grossly overshadowed by Clara Driscoll's money and by the DRT insistence that Clara was the sole savior of the Alamo. It is doubtful money alone could have saved the Alamo. Adina De Zavala did the hard work of saving the landmark, the research, the negotiations with Hugo and Schmeltzer, the building of a network of support for preservation. When she began her efforts, Clara Driscoll was still a child.

Adina De Zavala deserves to be celebrated as a historian, a teacher, and a woman. History does not have to decide if this complex woman was passionate about her cause or personally ambitious.

Adina continued her fight to preserve history and historical sites in Texas. She lived to be ninety-three and worked, even in the hospital, until she slipped into a coma from which she never awoke.

Inevitably, stories of the supernatural grew up around the deserted buildings of the mission complex based on both history and folklore. Strange ghostly sightings and tales of mysterious phenomena were part of the buildings' lore almost from the moment of the siege.

Mexican general Juan José de Andrade was in charge of the fortification of San Antonio de Béxar at the time of Santa Anna's defeat at San Jacinto. When Vincente Filisola took over command in Santa Anna's place, he ordered Andrade to evacuate his troops from the city. The story is told that, before leaving, Andrade told his men to destroy the Alamo. The way Adina Emilia De Zavala repeated the legend in her book, *History and Legends of the Alamo and Other Missions in and around San Antonio*, Andrade's troops were met with ghostly spirits with flaming swords and driven off before they could do much damage.

Superstitious residents of San Antonio through the years also believed that there were a series of underground passages beneath the Alamo and other missions. These passages were inhabited by "good people" who made appearances now and then. These "good people" did not stay in any one area but could suddenly appear on any part of the mission grounds, underlining the underground passage theory. Some were particularly active during stormy weather. Young children in San Antonio were encouraged to watch for the padre, a very old man who brought gifts because he needed money or a deed to land. There were also reports of sightings of a mysterious woman who once gave a young girl old Spanish coins and diamonds—the help the girl's family needed to seek medical help for her father, who had been injured in an Indian battle.

Perhaps the most haunting of the eerie legends surrounding the "good people" of the underground is that of the Woman in Blue. Once a generation, the Woman in Blue comes out of the dark passages of the Alamo to find recipient worthy of her gifts—always a woman. Said to be a native Texian, the woman is reportedly tall with gray eyes, and dark hair, but her age is indeterminate—she could be young or old. The gift she bestows is the ability to see to the heart of things with a clear vision of good or ill. And the recipient is to use her gift for the good of the people of her city and state, particularly the children.

Adina included the "Woman in Blue" in *History and Legends of the Alamo* but there is little mention of the story in other Alamo sources, and Adina may have included it in an attempt to incorporate into Alamo history the more widespread legend of the Woman in Blue of the American Southwest. That legend refers to Maria Jesus de Agreda of the Franciscan Poor Clares Convent, in Spain. María de Jesús de Agreda never left the Spanish convent and yet she was said to have ministered to natives in various parts of the American Southwest. Always clothed in brilliant blue, she traveled in spirit—or by what the church eventually recognized as "teleportation." The story is one of the most enduring legends of America's desert country, and it makes a fitting tale to add to the enduring legend of the Alamo.

CHAPTER EIGHT

———————•••———————

Clara Driscoll and the Limits of Philanthropy

After the 1908 debacle when Adina barricaded herself in the long barracks, Clara Driscoll's involvement in preservation efforts and the affairs of the DRT was sporadic. Back in New York, Clara either handled DRT and Alamo affairs long distance or, more often, left things up to the DRT members in San Antonio. She was not actually present for much of the ongoing conflict between the two DRT factions between 1908 and 1911, although she made occasional gifts for improvements to the property and she certainly heard about the goings-on from her friends in San Antonio.

Although she made occasional trips to Texas, she was ensconced in her New York home and social life. She and Hal entertained lavishly, and their home was a magnet for celebrities and international figures.

Back home, there was some resentment of her sudden rise to fame. Even some members of the DRT thought that Clara had ridden their hard preservation work to stardom, and there are suggestions her literary career might not have blossomed had she not already had the reputation as the Savior of the Alamo.

She did return to San Antonio for Governor Colquitt's 1911 hearing on the long barracks, at which her wish to destroy the barracks was soundly defeated. Some have said it was the only time in her life that

Clara Driscoll giving a speech, date and occasion unknown. San Antonio Light / San Antonio Express-News / ZUMA Press.

someone said "no" to Clara Driscoll. Governor Colquitt's decision went counter to popular belief at the time. Most people believed that the battle had taken place in the chapel and that it, not the colorless former convent, was the symbol of liberty. Historians play with the question of why Clara changed her mind, when she was once so willing to save the long barracks in which she invested her own money. Part of the answer may be that she was swayed by public opinion.

But as far back as 1905, Clara had made her intention clear. She expressly told the legislature that she bought the land for a beautiful memorial park to highlight the shrine of the Alamo. Probably she never intended to save the long barracks but saw Adina's path to purchasing the property as the first step toward realizing her vision of a park. Adina all along had envisioned a museum in the restored barracks, and Clara may well have gone along with that vision initially. At some point, she even had architect's drawings of the park she planned—a low wall with arched Spanish gateways replacing the long barracks in the drawing.

A careful reading of Clara's published short stories also gives a clue. The text of "The Custodian of the Alamo" refers to the chapel, where "the last stand was made," stating that Bowie was killed in the baptistry (he actually died in a room on the second floor of the convent), and refers to clearing away "that old building," meaning the barracks. In her fiction, she spoke the truth of her ambitions for the mission.

In the eyes of the public and particularly the tunnel vision of her chapter of the DRT, Clara remained the "Savior of the Alamo." The belief persisted, too, that Clara bought the property with her own money; the story of the state's reimbursement was often overlooked, and the DRT did little to correct the misconception. To add to the confusion of facts, the public generally believed that Clara bought the chapel, which in public eyes was the Alamo. In reality, she made the down payment that saved the long barracks. The state owned the chapel.

The headquarters of the Texas Federation of Women's Clubs. Clara Driscoll paid off the mortgage and gave the organization the deed to the building. Library of Congress.

The ugly battles and rumors within the DRT never tarnished Clara's reputation, and her DRT sisters worked hard to maintain it. When the members of the former De Zavala chapter put a plaque on the long barracks, extolling Adina's importance in saving the Alamo, the DRT covered the plaque and put one up crediting Clara Driscoll.

There is an irony in the complete credit given Clara for saving the Alamo. It was not the chapel she saved—the building that remains the public symbol of the battle—and she saved the building she wanted to destroy. History sometimes plays jokes on its participants.

Clara's absence from Texas ended in 1914. The Seviers followed a California trip with a stop in Texas to see her beloved father. He died during their visit and was laid to rest in the mausoleum he had so carefully planned.

Clara and Hal moved back to Texas, so that she could be near her brother, with whom she was close, and so that she could help with the family's sprawling business interests. Although the Driscoll businesses were headquartered in Corpus Christi, the couple chose to live in Austin, the state capital, where Hal would found the *Austin American* newspaper, also serving as editor. Clara began her philanthropic work in Texas almost immediately; one of the first projects she supported was the 1915 improvement of the public park in Refugio that holds a monument to Captain Aaron King, a hero of the Texas Revolution who died trying to evacuate families from Goliad and punish Mexicans and Karankawa Indians who were raiding deserted homes. But her main preoccupation was building a grand home in Austin on a piece of land at the foot of Mount Bonnell, overlooking the Colorado River. The Seviers had fallen in love with Lake Como on their honeymoon trip to Italy, and they found the spot they chose for their Texas home to be every bit as romantic and peaceful.

The land also appealed to Clara's deep interest in Texas history, as it had once belonged to Stephen F. Austin, the *empresario* and founder known as the "Father of Texas." Austin had planned to build his home there but died before he could carry out his wish.

Clara wanted a home that would have the style and feel of the Lake Como region that she loved—but she wanted it also to fit into its place in the Texas Hill Country. The couple designated architect Harvey L. Page of San Antonio to build them a Mediterranean-style mansion on the land. Coincidentally or not, Page had also been the architect who designed an elaborate amusement palace to be built at the northeast corner of the Alamo chapel and a garden to replace the long barracks when the destruction of that building seemed inevitable.

For the Seviers' home, which would be completed in 1917, Page designed a fifteen-room mansion on four levels, with a ballroom and a tower that could be seen for miles. The Seviers filled its spacious rooms with treasures from all over the world—rare books and paintings, copper and brass from the Orient, a desk with inlaid gold-leaf ornamentation and a matching chest from Florence, porcelain, French china, fine crystal, and antique silver. The Alamo was not left behind—the chapel was depicted in a carving over a fireplace.

Always interested in gardens, Clara designed formal gardens with an Italian fountain, rare gates, a sundial, a birdbath, and other statuary. Five acres of the land were landscaped; the remaining thirteen acres, wooded with mostly old post oaks, were left in the natural state. Four terraces looked out on these gardens. Clara also requested a copy of a window in San Antonio's Mission San José. The legend behind the window tells of a sculptor enamored of a young woman named Rosa who was lost at sea making her way from Spain to her lover in Texas, a tale that would have found a home in one of Clara's romantic and tragic love stories.[16]

Again harking back to her ranch background and her fiction, Clara named her new home *Laguna Gloria*, the name of one of the Driscoll ranches and a gentle reminder of her novel, *The Girl from La Gloria*.[17] *Laguna Gloria* soon outshone her Long Island home as a gathering place for international celebrities and dignitaries.

The Seviers liked entertaining and were gracious and easy hosts. They loved to open their home for large groups, and everyone from the DRT to the Democratic Party and even the Texas legislature held events at *Laguna Gloria*. Many of the big-name bands of the day entertained the sparkling guests at these festivities.

At about the same time construction on *Laguna Gloria* was completed, Hal began a career of public service. President Woodrow Wilson tapped him to chair the committee to disseminate public information in Argentina and Chile in an effort to counter right-wing German propaganda, which seemed to be spreading in South America in the aftermath of the Great War. No doubt Wilson chose Sevier because the two had been classmates at Princeton. Whether the Seviers spent the entire two years of Hal's service in South America or traveled there frequently is uncertain, but Clara supported Hal in his work. On the Seviers return to Texas, she established the Austin chapter of the Pan American Round Table, a group that raises funds to support students in Latin American Studies.

Life in Austin went along smoothly for the Seviers from 1917, when their home was completed, until 1929, when the world changed; the only ripple in their existence was the absence from Austin when Hal was appointed to responsibilities in South America. In the early years of the Seviers' return to Austin, Clara became a dedicated and active member of the Democratic Party. In her thesis on Adina De Zavala and Tejano heritage, Suzanne Seifert Cottraux sees Clara's insistence on demolishing the long barracks as the first manifestation of her ambition to be active in the Democratic Party. She made an annual generous donation to the party, sponsored balls, dinners, and other events. And in 1928 she was named Committee Woman from Texas, a post she held until a year or two before her death in 1945. Clara campaigned for Democrat Al Smith, the first Catholic presidential candidate, in 1928, when he lost to the Republican Herbert Hoover. She then campaigned for the ticket of Franklin Delano Roosevelt and John Nance Garner, though at the end of FDR's second term, when Cactus Jack Garner challenged him for the Democratic nomination, she supported Garner.

In 1929, Robert Driscoll died of complications from an amputation of a leg. Although her brother was ten years her elder, Clara felt they were good friends, and he had often relied on her advice as he managed the family's growing properties. Upon Robert's death, Clara was not only the sole surviving member of her family, she was also challenged with maintaining the family's complicated business affairs and stepping into Robert's shoes as an active member of the civic community in Corpus Christi. Because of the increasing need for her presence in Corpus Christi, the Seviers essentially closed up *Laguna Gloria* and moved to the Gulf Coast. Over the next years, Clara visited the Austin mansion occasionally but in 1943 donated it to the Texas Fine Arts Association.

Donating *Laguna Gloria* was a wrench for Clara. She wrote that she never wanted to sell the home in which she lived. "We perhaps forget that the founders of Texas were men of education and taste. . . . Texas has given a number of very good artists to the nation, Wayman Adams is one; Onderdonk of San Antonio, another. . . . In order to prove my interest in establishing a permanent art gallery here, I am glad to make this gift."

In 1995, *Laguna Gloria* became the Austin Museum of Art.

In Corpus Christi, Clara oversaw an estate of a hundred thousand acres, sixteen active oil wells, three gas wells, ranches, farms, a cotton gin, and diverse real estate holdings. Clara was also president and sole owner of the Corpus Christi Bank & Trust, the owner of a chain of hotels, and a shareholder in equities in such huge monopolies as the Taft syndicate. Following Robert's example of promoting the economic development of South Texas and Corpus Christi, in particular, she took on such projects as the establishment of a naval base outside Corpus Christi and the development of once-barren Padre Island as a seaside playground.

The Driscoll companies were headquartered in the bank owned by the family. And Clara, who went by her maiden name for business purposes, spent much of her time there. If she was intimidated by the challenge of managing the vast Driscoll estate, it was not for long. She was soon recognized as an outstanding businesswoman. Under her leadership, the assets of the Corpus Christi Bank & Trust increased by $13 million in twelve years. Still, she managed to continue her political activities and her life as a clubwoman.

The Seviers' entertaining at the Driscoll family home on the ranch was less spectacular than it had been at *Laguna Gloria*. They split their time between hotel suites in town and the ranch, which was twenty-some miles away. Still, one year they hosted the annual convention of the DRT in Corpus Christi and provided a tour of the Rio Grande Valley in chartered buses and private cars.

A woman of incredible energy and constant activity for her entire life, Clara found some respite and relaxation at the family Palo Alto ranch. It was, she said, peaceful and quiet. She could take a stack of unopened mail and a good book with her to the old family home, and once there she enjoyed spending quiet time catching up on her reading and walking with her pack of Russian wolfhounds.

In 1933, Hal was called back to public service when he was appointed ambassador to Chile by President Franklin D. Roosevelt. A persistent rumor had it that FDR, an early proponent of women's service, first offered the position to Clara, but that she demurred in favor of her husband. Sevier's official nomination to the post, made by the Texas legislature, included a statement to the effect that his "brilliant and distinguished wife" would reflect added credit on this appointment. In reality, Roosevelt probably had Hal in mind for the post all along because of his previous experience in South America. Clara, however, was a prominent supporter of the Democratic Party and FDR—more so than her husband.

The couple left their business arrangements in the hands of employees and directors of the various Driscoll enterprises and made the move to Chile It was the first time that control of Driscoll enterprises had not been in family hands since Clara's father's time, and Clara would later have cause to regret the move for business reasons. But the Seviers also found that Chile had changed dramatically from what they had known at the end of World War I. The aristocracy no longer ruled the country, and a strong middle class had emerged as an active force. Still, much about Chile was backward, including its agricultural infrastructure. Farms there could not feed the population because they were mired in old technology. However, mining was an important industry, and vineyards were beginning to produce credible wine. Regardless of the growth of mining and wine making, however, the Chilean economy was weak, also feeling the effects of the worldwide depression that had taken hold, particularly in the United States. Social disorder prevailed at all levels. Unfortunately, Hal proved a disappointment as an ambassador, and many of his duties fell to Clara. For one thing, Hal's Spanish was halting at best; she was fluent in the language. Hal was genial and made friends easily, but he had little concept of either the official duties of an ambassador or the governmental workings of Chile, despite his earlier experience there. Amid rumors of his ill health, after two years he resigned his post, and the couple returned to Texas.

By the time of their return to Corpus Christi, the Sevier marriage had been plagued by discord for some time, though both parties were discreetly quiet about their marital troubles. Back at home on the Gulf Coast, they took separate suites in a hotel and were rarely seen together. Rumors about their marital state were rife, of course, given that they were such a high-profile couple.

When the marriage finally broke up, Clara blamed Hal's immoderate consumption of alcohol for their estrangement. Ever since their honeymoon, Clara had been concerned about Hal's drinking, and his addiction was offered as a concrete cause of their split. Hal may also have indulged in occasional affairs, though there is little hard historical evidence. It may also well be that Clara simply lost respect for him after his dismal performance in Chile. Success, after all, meant a lot to Clara.

Even though the couple had been unhappy and living essentially separate lives for some time, Clara's 1935 filing for divorce caught him by surprise.

"I have no comment until I talk to my wife," he told reporters who cornered him when the news became public. Clara, for her part, would have nothing to do with the clamoring reporters, simply claiming that she was indisposed. At one point, Clara's staff even issued a statement that she was unavailable due to a recent heart attack, but no such event has been verified.

The final divorce, not granted until 1937, cited incompatibility and mental cruelty as its causes, which leaves room for almost anything. The delay may have been due to attempts at reconciliation. But in the end, it was a clean break. There were no children, and virtually no community property, since their lifestyles had mostly been supported by the Driscoll fortunes. According to rumor, Hal tried unsuccessfully to prove that some assets were jointly acquired. Clara offered him a generous settlement, which he at first declined and then accepted. He moved back to Tennessee and died in 1940, a relatively poor man.

When the divorce was final, Clara officially took back her maiden name and went on with her life. The DRT named her honorary President for Life—she had most recently served as state president from 1927 to 1931. The Texas Federation of Women's Clubs followed suit and held an elaborate celebration, called Clara Driscoll Day, in 1939, which included the unveiling of a life-size portrait of Clara in their Austin headquarters, a Georgian Revival mansion designed by Dallas architect Henry Coke Knight. When the federation nearly lost its new Austin clubhouse, due to poor financial arrangements, Clara refinanced the property at an extremely favorable rate and later wrote off the debt completely.

Clara was often the subject of elaborate tributes and even several poems. She followed the family pattern of contributing to civic projects in Corpus Christi and was particularly interested in attracting tourists, taking an active part in the development of Padre Island. A devout Catholic, she also founded the Catholic Education League. Its first project was the construction of a Catholic women's dormitory on the campus of the University of Texas in Austin.

While Clara seemed celebrated as an outstanding woman of Texas for all her contributions, she also had a major defeat. Her brother Robert had built a hotel on the bluff above downtown Corpus Christi, and Clara inherited control of that property along with the rest of Robert's estate. But while the Seviers were in Chile, control of that specific property had passed to the mayor of San Antonio, a man who was not in Clara's favor. Upon her return to Corpus Christi, she brought suit to have the hotel returned to her control, but the judgment went against her.

An apocryphal story is that she attempted to stay at the hotel.

"I'm sorry, ma'am, but we're full," the room clerk said.

"Call your manager," Clara told him imperiously.

When the manager arrived, he repeated the clerk's words. "I'm sorry, but we really are all full."

Clara took a deep breath. "Do you know who I am?"

The manager shook his head, and she identified herself.

"I'm sorry, Mrs. Driscoll, but we really don't have any unoccupied rooms."

Clutching her purse in indignation, she turned away but not before saying, "Fine. I'll build my own hotel so that I can look down on you."

And she did—right next door and two stories taller. Clara named it the Robert Driscoll Hotel.[18] She occupied the penthouse for several years, looking down on the hotel that had denied her.

For President Roosevelt's third inauguration in 1940, Clara took the Hardin Simmons University thirty-six-piece Cowboy Band to Washington, D.C., along with six white horses ridden by college girls, to participate in the parade. In 1944, however, she resigned as Committee Woman from Texas. She may have been tired of the stressful *Sturm und Drang* of politics, especially during the war years, but also her health was failing. She had served in that role sixteen years, thereby setting a longevity record for the position.

By 1944, the sixty-three-year-old was not just showing her age, she was clearly ill. An auto accident suffered years earlier had resulted in an injury that now flared up, causing her to limp. Eventually she resorted to a wheelchair. Clara Driscoll spent her last days in the penthouse of her new hotel, mostly alone except for Spots, a fox terrier she doted on. She was partially reclusive, disillusioned, with no close friends, no confidantes, and attended only by a nurse and a maid. She died of a stroke on July 17, 1945, at the age of sixty-four. Her body lay in state in the Alamo chapel before she, too, went to join her family in the mausoleum.

Just as Adina later died without family or friends to take over her preservationist work, Clara Driscoll died with no one to take the reins of her businesses or to perpetuate her philanthropy. The Driscoll Foundation Children's Hospital in Corpus Christi received the majority of her vast estate. The hospital treats crippled, maimed, and diseased Texas children whose parents cannot afford medical care.

The hospital sold Clara's personal effects which, surprisingly, contained only a few pictures of her—she was apparently camera shy. At auction, the hospital foundation sold items ranging from glass, porcelain, and Oriental brass to cast-iron pots and kettles from the ranch and a small collection of swords and firearms. The ranch land was also part of the estate, and hospital authorities set aside ninety acres, mostly farmland, for the Driscoll Boys City. Estimates of the value of the estate were between $4 and $7 million; income from the estate covered the operating expenses of the hospital.

West elevation. Library of Congress, Historic American Building Survey, April 1938. Arthur W. Stewart, photographer.

In 1978, the state unveiled an Official Texas Historical Marker honoring Clara Driscoll in front of the Driscoll Mausoleum in San Antonio's Alamo Masonic Cemetery.

Clara Driscoll was many things—a ranch woman, a preservationist, a celebrity. A writer once described her as a "fiery redhead, [who] could ride, fight, drink and swear with the gusto of a cowpuncher." Other historians have discounted the idea that she could or would fight, drink, or swear. And though proud of her ranching heritage, as she aged, she apparently considered the ranching life "unladylike."

Adina De Zavala was present in San Antonio for all the campaign to save the Alamo, specifically the long barracks. Much of Clara Driscoll's part of the battle was waged long distance, and yet history until recently has overlooked Adina's role and given sole credit to Clara for the preservation effort. Newspapers across the country spread Clara's reputation as the "Savior of the Alamo" and the DRT picked up on the theme, repeating it for almost a century. Clara herself never demurred and pointed out that Adina also deserved recognition, though she must be given credit for offering to resign at the DRT meeting in Galveston where things did not go her way. Giving equal credit to Adina should in no way diminish Clara's importance in providing the needed money.

For all the years since the second Battle of the Alamo, the DRT kept the legend of Clara as the Savior of the Alamo alive. Without the efforts of the organization, however, Clara Driscoll might be as little known as her once-friend and then rival Adina De Zavala. Clara kept no personal record of the events of the time, and all that history knows about her participation comes from the words of others. Her celebrity was brief and fleeting—as an author, an ambassador's wife, a hostess. She was a philanthropist, first and foremost, though philanthropy was intensely personal with her. She gave to causes she cared about. The Alamo was the only preservation project she ever supported.

Some Forgotten Texas Heroines

If Adina De Zavala is the overlooked heroine of the second Battle of the Alamo, she joins a couple of interesting ladies from the Battle of the Alamo and the Texas war for independence.

Cat Jennings of Bastrop was the daughter of the oldest man to die at the Alamo. After hearing of her father's death, the fourteen-year-old mounted her horse and rode alone across Austin's Colony, urging men to join Houston's ragged army and fight for Texas. Cat's great-great-great-granddaughter swears it's true, but she can't find the newspaper clipping she once had about that famous ride. Who knows? But it makes a great story.

Pamela Mann might better be called a villain for her oddly funny part in Texas history. Headed for San Jacinto, Houston stopped at the Groce Plantation to train his troops. While there he confiscated two oxen to pull the cannon he had somehow obtained. He assured the good woman he planned to turn east, toward Nacogdoches and safety; instead, he turned toward Harrisburg and the Mexican Army. When Mrs. Mann heard this, she followed Houston and demanded her oxen back, blocking his horse so Houston could not escape.

Houston refused, and she pulled out a knife and slashed the leather strips binding the animals to the cannon. Brandishing a whip, she drove them away.

When the wagon master told Houston he couldn't pull the cannon without oxen and was going after her, Houston supposedly said, "Well, good luck. You'll need it. That woman will fight."

Legend has it that the wagon master returned, late at night, limping, his shirt in shreds, refusing to talk about what happened. But he didn't have the oxen.

CHAPTER NINE

———•◦•———

The Alamo of the Imagination

Unwittingly, Adina and Clara, by saving the Alamo, laid the foundation for an entire branch of the entertainment industry. If the Alamo had not been preserved and celebrated in San Antonio as a symbol of Texas independence, it is doubtful that the story of its historic battle would have fired the imagination of everyone from movie stars and authors to balladeers and the designers of playsets. These creative imaginations have kept the Alamo legend alive in countless movies and books and even a body of poetry. It is movies, however, that often shape our idea of the story, for better or, more often, worse, and it is ironic that the chapel building's famous façade is most often the face of the movies, books, and other representations of the site.

While the Alamo story has been dramatically acted out on the big and little screen numerous times, none of the productions has been a notable success. As Alamo historian Frank Thompson points out, the story is not well suited to cinematic treatment. If the movie were to be about the actual battle, it would be fairly short, so most include the thirteen-day siege, and sieges by their very nature are a matter of waiting. Tense, perhaps for those under siege, but boring for a movie audience. And there is little tension, because the audience already knows how the story ends. They are just waiting for the good guys to be slaughtered.

The classic film version of the story is John Wayne's 1959 movie *The Alamo*. Wayne thought, planned, and dreamed of this project for ten years. It would be his first "big" movie, and he wanted to be sure it was done right and not on the cheap, but he faced several problems, such as how to finance it, where to shoot it, and which actors should play key roles.

Wayne's first challenge was to find a location, and he was on the lookout everywhere he went, whether on location for a film or traveling as a private individual. Twice he decided to shoot in Mexico, but the prejudice against Mexicans as the demon soldiers who killed the glorious defenders immediately cropped up as an objection to filming there. Advisors told Wayne a Mexican location was a really bad idea. The DRT, always eager to control the narrative, went further and told him the movie would not be shown in Texas theaters if it was filmed in Mexico. No one knows if the DRT had the power to enforce that threat or not, but they seemed to think they were still the conservators of the Alamo story as well as the property.

In the mid-1950s, Happy Shahan approached Wayne and offered his property in Brackettville, Texas, *Happy Shahan's HV Ranch*, as a possible location for the film. The set that was built there was constructed to Wayne's specifications, at three-quarters of the original property's size. Unfortunately, in Brackettville, there were no trees in sight, and in the movie version, the mission sat on a barren Texas plain instead of a river setting with cottonwood trees lining the bank.

Financial problems plagued the project, delaying it beyond Wayne's hoped-for release date. Director John Ford, although not personally involved in the project, decreed that Wayne should play Davy Crockett, an American folk hero, after the release of the film *Davy Crockett, King of the Wild Frontier* in 1955. The lead song from that movie was on everyone's lips, particularly children who now sported coonskin caps. Having John Wayne play Crockett would draw moviegoers in droves.

Northwest elevation of the chapel. Library of Congress, Historic American Building Survey, April 1938. Arthur W. Stewart, photographer.

The rest of cast was also star-studded: Richard Widmark as Bowie; Laurence Harvey as Travis; Joan O'Brien as Susanna Dickinson; Richard Boone as Houston; and Ruben Padilla as Santa Anna. Frankie Avalon, Patrick Wayne, and Chill Wills also had roles in the film.

Although the movie was passed over for an Academy Award, reviews praised it as spectacular, overwhelming, breathtaking, and "Texas Terrific." Some called it an outstanding accomplishment for Wayne, who produced, directed, and starred. Critics were not so kind, calling it historically "hit or miss," a vanity project for Wayne, and in the words of film critic Christopher Null, "wildly overwrought, clumsy, and embarrassingly directed."

A 2004 remake of the movie opened to negative advance reviews, but many reviewers praised the new version for capturing the scope and depth of the battle with historical accuracy. Renowned critic Roger Ebert gave it high praise, saying it "captures the loneliness and dread of men waiting for ... certain death" and saying it succeeds in "taking popular culture heroes like Davy Crockett and Jim Bowie and giving them human form."

Wayne's film was certainly not the first attempt to capture the story on screen. The 1911 film *The Immortal Alamo* begins the story a century or more before the battle, with the establishment of the mission system, while the 1915 *Martyrs of the Alamo* sticks pretty much to the event itself. The 1937 film, *Heroes of the Alamo* is a straight forward retelling of the battle story and reuses scenes from a 1926 silent film.

Some movies seemed to want to capitalize on the popular appeal of the Alamo, using the word in the title even when the film had little to do with the battle. The 1953 movie *The Man from the Alamo,* starring Glenn Ford, even sent a supposed survivor of the massacre to restore peace in Ox Bow, North Dakota.

One film that stands out is the 1987 TV production *Thirteen Days to Glory*, written by journalist Lon Tinkle and based on his book by that title. James Arness starred as Jim Bowie, with Brian Keith as Davy Crockett and Alec Baldwin as William Barrett Travis. One reviewer's headline perhaps says it all: "Good Intentions Don't Always Make Great Films." Another reviewer praises the movie's attempt once again to cast the story in human terms but calls it seriously miscast.

Another movie offers yet a different battle for the Alamo, this one a spoof. The 1968 movie *Viva Max!* is the story of a Mexican general whose girlfriend scorns him by telling him his men would not follow him to a whorehouse. To prove her wrong, the general leads his men into Texas to retake the Alamo. In their haste, they forget their guns. The Texas Rangers come out to defend the Alamo, but they are forbidden to use guns by the government, which does not want bloodshed. Based on the book by James Lehrer, the movie is one big joke, which upset the DRT. They supported Wayne but tried to stop filming of *Viva Max!* One DRT member was heard to moan, "Why couldn't they make a nice movie like Mr. Wayne did?"

In the 1950s, when *Davy Crockett, King of the Wild Frontier* inspired a Crockett craze, toy companies, like the famous Marx company, scrambled to create products for the market. Marx was so taken off guard by the demand that their first playset rushed into production. "Davy Crockett at the Alamo" featured soldiers from Fort Dearborn fighting Indians in front of the Alamo. The company soon corrected that, replacing the soldiers and Indians with authentic defenders and Mexican soldiers in later versions. Other companies followed the craze by producing their own playsets of varying quality and authenticity. The craze petered out rather quickly, but some playsets were available into the late seventies or early eighties. Today, those children's toys are highly prized by collectors.

Jigsaw puzzles about the Alamo appeared as early as 1920, and the Crockett movie also inspired some board games, notably Davy Crockett's Alamo Game, which required players to answer such questions as "Who first led American settlers into Texas?" or "What is Deguello?" The Battle of the Alamo game came with the advice that contrary to history, the defenders could win at this game.

Although many movies of the day inspired promotional items such as games, puzzles, comics, and books, John Wayne did not accompany his film with a merchandising campaign. Perhaps he felt the Crockett merchandise had exhausted the audience. Music from the movie did catch on, however, with recordings of "Remember the Alamo," "The Ballad of the Alamo," and "The Green Leaves of Summer," by various artists.

Today you can also order coonskin caps online and occasionally find action figures, usually plastic, of the Alamo defenders and Mexican soldiers, and even playsets with plastic models of the chapel—though usually without the ramparts or firing platforms of the long barracks. Jigsaw puzzles, usually replicating familiar paintings of the scene, are available, and a site called boardgamegeek.com offers Alamo-themed board games.

All of these imaginative adaptations would have drawn a frown—or more probably sharp words—from both Adina and Clara. Adina would

The nave (looking west), showing the original doors to the Veramundi House (Spanish Governor's Palace). Library of Congress, Historic American Building Survey, 1961.

have despaired for their historical inaccuracy and Clara would have believed they besmirched the shrine to Texas heroes. However, both women might reluctantly agree that by making fun games and toys of the story of the Alamo, the event was imprinted in big and little minds. One could only hope that the truth would take over the romanticizing.

Books about the Alamo—the actual event and not the Wayne movie— have had more success and enjoyed a longer shelf life. There are almost countless nonfiction studies of the Alamo and the massacre, some good, some not so good.

Fiction about the Alamo is much scarcer. A novel that received good attention when published in 2000 is Stephen Harrigan's *The Gates of the Alamo*, which follows three fictional characters as they are drawn into the siege and the battle. A huge, sprawling, and complex novel, it occasionally tells the story from the viewpoint of the attacking Mexican soldiers.

Some authors of good reputation have written books about the Alamo aimed at the young-adult reader, but these too are almost all nonfiction. They include John Jakes's *Susanna of the Alamo*, the story of Mrs. Dickinson, purportedly the only Anglo woman in the mission during the massacre, and *Battle of the Alamo* by Texas author and publisher Bryce Milligan with illustrations by the late Charles Shaw. *Remembering the Alamo* by prolific young-adult author Alicia A. Willis is fiction, but it's a contemporary story about a pastor who takes a youth group to the shrine and runs into unexpected trouble. Renowned southern novelist Robert Penn Warren also wrote a young-adult book, appropriately titled *Remember the Alamo*, published in 1958.

Who knows in what directions creative imaginations will take the Alamo story in the future? Because of Adina and Clara, the story lives on.

CHAPTER TEN

The Twenty-First Century and a Third Battle of the Alamo

W e may well see the third Battle of the Alamo. Battle lines have been drawn, and once again it will be a battle of image versus history.

The DRT has long been criticized for mismanagement of the Alamo site, dating back almost to when Governor Colquitt gave stewardship of the mission to the organization. Having wrested control of the long barracks from both Adina De Zavala and the State of Texas but yet thwarted in their plans to demolish it and create a memorial park, the DRT simply did nothing with the structure except to ignore it for fifty long years. It was roofless, floorless, deserted, and decaying. Then San Antonio began planning for the 1968 Hemisfair.

Various nations have hosted world fairs or international exhibitions since the French began the tradition in the mid-nineteenth century. These fairs showcase the achievements not just of the host nation but all nations who care to participate. The Columbian Exposition held in Chicago in 1893 may be the best known of those on American soil. In that tradition, in 1968, San Antonio held an international exhibit with the theme "The Confluence of Cultures in the Americas." The exposition also marked the 250th anniversary of the founding of the city.

The exposition grounds were built on ninety-two acres at the edge of downtown, land that had once been farmed by residents of the San Antonio Mission de Valero. The area was considered one of urban blight, and the existing structures and land plots were mostly obtained under the right of eminent domain.

Hired in the early 1960s, renowned San Antonio architect Ford O'Neil was primary architect for the project, but his contract was ended two years before the 1968 opening, probably because his plan called for saving 120 out of the 129 buildings in the area slated for destruction that had been designated by preservationists as historically important. Ultimately, twenty-four of the historic buildings were retained. The San Antonio River Walk was extended to link to a lagoon within the fair grounds. This network of parks and sidewalks along the banks of the San Antonio River is lined with shops and restaurants and is a major tourist attraction for the city of San Antonio. Today, the exposition site is known as Hemisfair Park, and several of the pavilions remain standing, preserved for history. The most notable structure is the 750-foot-tall Tower of the Americas, which has a revolving restaurant and an observation deck at the top.

The exposition was expected to draw thousands of international visitors to San Antonio, and preparations were citywide. As part of the exposition, the DRT, forbidden to demolish the long barracks, chose to renovate the structure and turn it into a museum, which still operates today.

Four other missions survive in San Antonio, preserved in the San Antonio Mission National Park. These missions serve as centers for the Latino community, offering religious services and festivals, such as the annual Day of the Dead celebrations. These missions help preserve the Latino heritage of the area in contrast to the prevailing white, European history. One of Adina's accomplishments, conscious or not, in preserving the missions was to call attention to her city's multiethnic heritage.

Front (west) façade. Library of Congress, Historic American Building Survey, 1961.

Adina De Zavala would not recognize the Alamo site today; Clara Driscoll would probably rejoice that at least some of her dreams have come true. Today, the plaza stands almost as the compromise the two women never reached in life, fulfilling parts of each of their visions. The chapel has been restored, its façade redesigned with the now famous "hump" that in the eyes of most is the centerpiece of any image of the Alamo. The chapel is a hallowed place, where visitors are asked to remove their hats and lower their voices. What remains of the long barracks is almost entirely reconstructed. In the renovation following Governor Colquitt's 1911 decision, the back wall of the building was rebuilt, with few pieces remaining of the original. Souvenir stores and fast-food restaurants stand where the west wall of the mission once stood, a post office replaced the north wall where Travis fired the cannon and died, and the "low barracks" is now a park.

For many visitors, the first reaction to the site is "It's so small!" They expect a fort that stands clear, away from the hustle and bustle of downtown, with battlements and cannons, and all the marks of a raging battle; they find a quiet, symbolic place at the center of city life. Two to three million tourists a year visit the Alamo and bring the city of San Antonio upwards of $8 billion dollars in revenues.

Additional buildings have been added to the complex since Hemisfair: The DRT Library was added in 1950; there is an auditorium and a DRT museum and gift shop separate from that in the long barracks. A "Wall of History" beside the museum gives an overview of the mission before and after the battle. Landscaping that might have met even Harvey Page's critical approval is evident throughout the grounds.

Particularly interesting is the cenotaph, a monument designed by none other than Pompeo Coppini, the sculptor who first alerted Adina to the impending sale of the barracks. This sixty-foot-tall monument is of gray Georgia marble set on a slab of Texas pink granite. The idealistic figure represents the spirit of sacrifice as exhibited by those who died defending the Alamo. Standing along the base are low-relief figures of the heroes—Crockett, Travis, Bowie, Bonham.

In 1984, a Chicago-area resident named Gary Foreman took on a crusade: to restore the original grounds of the mission, not just the chapel and long barracks but all the property that had since fallen into commercial hands. He claimed inspiration came to him one day as he was photographing the mission and was angered by the tourist attractions on the original grounds—Louis Tussaud's Wax Museum, Guinness World Records Museum, and Ripley's Believe It or Not! Odditorium.

Foreman was scorned by the DRT, among others, for being an outsider, a non-Texan who didn't understand the sacred nature of the shrine. Others, though, listened to him, including Fess Parker (the original Davy Crockett impersonator) and musician Phil Collins.

In 2006, Foreman produced a documentary, *Alamo Plaza: A Star Reborn*, which may well have been the catalyst for what looks like the third Battle of the Alamo.

If the third battle comes to blows, the cenotaph may be at the center of the fray. In 1994, San Antonio newspaper columnist David Richelieu proposed demolishing or moving all the buildings on the plaza, rebuilding parts of the mission within a new park. The plan included use of the first floor of the federal building as a museum, reconstruction of cannon platforms, and the installation of statues of historic figures, along with the closure of Alamo Plaza East, a small street next to the long barracks and the chapel. In effect, Richelieu was proposing Clara's vision all over again, calling for the church to stand "free and clear." Richelieu estimated the total cost of his elaborate plans at $32.6 million. A study group was formed, but few of the recommendations were enacted.

More than a decade later, in 2009, criticism of the DRT became intense. A series of mishaps—a failed 175th anniversary concert featuring Phil Collins, a known Alamo enthusiast and collector; calls for more oversight; and an investigation by the state attorney general—led to legislation ending the DRT's 106 years as sole custodian of the Alamo and gave the responsibility for the site to the Government Land Office. Governor Rick Perry signed the legislation into law, and the land office promptly contracted with the DRT for maintenance.

When George P. Bush, nephew of former President George W. Bush and son of former Florida governor Jeb Bush, was elected to head the land office in 2014, he took on a big project: fixing the Alamo. Bemoaning the current carnival atmosphere of the plaza, which offered cheesy tourist traps, including the wax figures that had offended Foreman, a bearded lady, and carny barkers, Bush also pointed out that vandalism was so common that the DRT had installed monitors and hired around-the-clock guard. He then laid out for the legislature the plan, first called "Reimagine the Alamo," which would dramatically tell the story of a world-renowned battle.

By that time, the west wall was totally gone, with only a remnant of the original foundation still intact. The old post office and federal building stood at the site of the north wall. Twentieth-century urban sprawl had nearly completed the destruction Santa Anna ordered in 1836.

Bush proposed a renovation project estimated to cost between $400 and $450 million. Plans included closing Alamo Street to vehicles, recreating the south and west walls, low barracks, and the defensive mound of earth and main gate, converting the existing post office to a multimedia center and museum, and most controversial of all, moving the cenotaph to the south end of the plaza, directly across from the Menger Hotel. Bush promised the project would trace the total history of the mission. The plan also called for only authentic materials—stone and adobe—to be used in rebuilding decayed sections such as the west wall. Perhaps the most laudable part of the plan called for emphasis on the role of Mexicans in the history of San Antonio and the Alamo. Introducing a note of controversy, however, his emphasis was on military uses of the site and not its earlier history as a mission.

Critics leaped on the plan immediately, claiming that it called for out-of-state "experts" who knew nothing about what the mission means to Texans to make the changes. Originally, the proposal called for a

Close-up of the main entrance to the chapel. Library of Congress, Historic American Building Survey, 1961.

plexiglass panel that showed where the walls stood in 1836, which residents thought would offer a jarring modern note. Moving the cenotaph, the monument honoring the fallen defenders, caused the most consternation. One woman likened it to moving the Tomb of the Unknown Soldier. Others said it would homogenize the site, putting twenty-first-century priorities over history—in other words, turning it into yet another theme park.

In 2015, Bush cancelled the maintenance agreement with the DRT, saying that the organization failed to keep the Alamo in good order and repair consistent with the age and condition of the complex; he retained control of the Alamo in the land office, where it was farmed out to outside managers. There was a call for an audit, questioning the use of public money without apparent oversight and failure to follow state laws. Politics became the battlefield, when Bush next ran for reelection.

Although at one point work on the proposed restoration and reimagining was expected to begin in 2016, the project stalled. Then in the fall of 2018, a citizens' review committee approved the plan and George P. Bush and the mayor of San Antonio signed an agreement to the plan as approved. The City of San Antonio would hold a fifty-year lease from the state, with two twenty-five-year extensions. Because of the lease, the mayor's signature was required on the agreement. After much controversy, work on the immense restoration project began in February 2019, with completion scheduled for 2024, the 300th anniversary of the mission in this location. The San Antonio City Council approved a $450 million renovation project, with the State of Texas committed to contribute $106 million, the city to provide $38 million, and the balance to come from private donations.

Where are the Defenders of the Alamo Memorialized?

One piece of the story of the defenders of the Alamo may always remain a mystery. Even though the land and buildings that remain on the Alamo Plaza have been preserved as a shrine to their memory, no one knows for sure what happened to the remains of those brave Texians. A year after the massacre, Colonel Juan Seguín returned to the Alamo to collect the ashes of the martyrs and give the remains a Christian burial. History does not record the location of the final resting place, and the actual whereabouts of the ashes has long been the subject of great controversy. Some say the ashes are buried in Fernando Cathedral, the mother church of the archdiocese of San Antonio, but others claim they were buried elsewhere in a common grave marked by a stone, which has since disappeared.

In 1936, workers at Fernando Cathedral did discover ashes buried under the floor in front of the altar rail. At the time it was not uncommon to bury the ashes of priests and a few others in that part of a church building. However, the Bishop of Fernando Cathedral immediately and without proof identified them as the ashes of the defenders, claiming even to have seen shreds of uniforms and tufts of reddish hair. Critics cited the improbability of remnants surviving either the fire or the passage of time before Seguín could have returned to see to the burial. San Antonio was still in Mexicans hands until Seguín took over the city in September, by which time weather would have scattered and destroyed the ashes.

According to an account that Seguín published in the Columbia *Telegraph and Texas Register*, he found three funeral pyres or piles of ashes and put two of them into an *urna* (coffin or casket), engraved on the inside lid with the names of Travis, Bowie, and Crockett, whose bones he speculated he had found among the others based on their placement at the site. The account goes on to describe a procession whereby the ashes seem to have been taken from the church to where they were originally found, honored by musket volleys, and reburied. But where?

Some scholars point to a modest plot with a stone plaque and obelisk in the Oddfellows Cemetery about a mile from the Alamo. Indeed, a historical marker on the Alamo grounds recounts the memory of an eight-year-old boy who recalled seeing the ashes dug up and transported to the Oddfellows Cemetery.

But late in life, a failing Seguín wrote a letter indicating placement of the urn with a "few fractions" of the ashes in a sepulcher at the cathedral. Historians have tended to discount the letter, given the state of Seguín's health at the time.

In his book *Lone Star*, published in 1968, noted Texas historian T. R. Fehrenbach flatly stated that the ashes were buried in a common grave and never found, a scenario far more likely than the Fernando Cathedral internment. It is also likely that the actual whereabouts of the defenders' remains will always be unknown.

EPILOGUE

---•••---

The Future of the Past

The Alamo would no doubt still stand today if Adina De Zavala and Clara Driscoll had not taken a hand with history, but it would probably be overwhelmed by urban crowding, with cheap stores marking its borders, perhaps a parking lot, certainly noisy motor vehicle traffic disturbing its solemn air of tranquility. No doubt, all remnants of the

Night at the Alamo. Carol Highsmith Collection, Library of Congress.

original mission would be gone and only the chapel left standing, and that might be in such poor repair that visitors could not safely enter.

But the two dedicated women did intervene, and in some sense, they changed Texas history. Certainly, they changed the general population's understanding of the battle and the massacre, and they brought historic preservation to prominence in San Antonio and in Texas, if not the whole country.

Together, Adina De Zavala and Clara Driscoll represented two qualities that many Texans respond to: heritage and money. Adina had the passion for historical accuracy; Clara had the money and the sense of drama. As a DRT member said at the time, neither could have saved the Alamo alone. Theirs was a natural union but hard-headedness—also a Texas trait—turned what was once a friendship into bitter rivalry. What is most sad is that their enmity extended beyond themselves to involve an organization and a lot of innocent women who were caught in the midst of an aesthetic battle.

Other battles may well loom in the future of the Alamo. A battle of words raged over the Alamo in 2018 when a committee of volunteers recommended to the State Board of Education that teachers be instructed to omit the word "heroic" in reference to the defenders. The reason given was that the word is value oriented. There may be any number of concepts behind that statement. Is it an attempt to recognize that the defenders were interlopers, not conquering heroes? Is it an attempt to counter the racism that has steadily increased in South Texas over the past century, portraying all people of color, but especially Mexicans, as somehow inferior to the pure white soldiers? Perhaps it's time to point more frequently to the stories of the many Mexicans who fought alongside Travis rather than against him.

The committee also suggested teachers might mention, but not teach, Travis's "Victory or Death" letter, but they did not distinguish the difference between mentioning and teaching. These recommendations were

Arcade of the new courtyard, looking north. Library of Congress, Historic American Building Survey, April 1938. Arthur W. Stewart, photographer.

part of "streamlining," which also eliminated Helen Keller and Hillary Rodham Clinton from the curriculum. And while these recommendations have since been countermanded, they reflect the conflict over interpretation that has plagued the history of the Alamo site for generations.

The Alamo has withstood several battles, many thanks to the two ladies whose stories are told on these pages. It will no doubt survive future battles to remain a significant, if controversial, monument to the rich history of Texas.

There are many versions of the Alamo story and of the events that surrounded the second battle. In part, what we know depends on whose version you listen to: Clara Driscoll's followers; those who were loyal to Adina De Zavala; bystanders and people who heard things secondhand. Historians have not settled on details of the Battle of the Alamo, even the number of men who died there, and probably never will because surviving records tell different stories. Too, there are several versions, with varying details, about Adina's barricade in the long barracks—more dramatic are the stories that she was without food, water, and lights; more probable, however, is the version by deputies at the scene that she had food, water, coffee, electricity, lights, and access to a telephone. Events at the raucous 1907 convention of the DRT cast blame in all directions, so one can't be sure of what happened. And so it goes. The reader is urged to use judgment—and maybe a dose of skepticism. Writers can't even agree on the color of Clara Driscoll's hair: while one describes her as a "fiery redhead," another mentions her jet-black hair. Where is truth?

But the second battle makes a darn good story.

NOTES

—————◦●●———————

1   Robert Ables, in his article on Adina's preservation work, "The Second Battle of the Alamo" (*Southwestern Historical Quarterly*, January 1967) places Coppini at the Menger with Adina when she met Clara, but no other sources support this.

2   There is little evidence for this destruction order in the historical record. Some historians think that Houston fabricated his destruction order, presenting it only after the siege and massacre took place.

3   Lorenzo de Zavala wrote his name with a lowercase "d"; Adina preferred to sign hers with the uppercase "D."

4   History tells us that Emily, the one in the tent with Santa Anna at San Jacinto, was taken in by a Texas soldier and remained in Texas until 1837 when she returned to her home in Connecticut. But an English journalist, William Bollaert, was so taken with her adventure that he told the story in his journal. It was picked up by other journalists and became part of Texas folklore, though many Texans will swear it's history. Band leader Mitch Miller popularized the song, "The Yellow Rose of Texas," and folklorist and journalist Frank Tolbert suggested that Emily Morgan was the girl in the song. There is an Emily Morgan Hotel in San Antonio, but no picture exists of the young mulatto woman.
"You may talk about your Clementine
And sing of Rosa Lee,
But the Yellow Rose of Texas
Is the only girl for me."

5   Lorenzo's letters, found in Adina's personal papers at the Center for American History, corroborate two famous paintings that hang in the Texas Capitol Building and appear to include a young Lorenzo Jr.

6   Now Sam Houston State University.

7   In 2019 dollars, this would be the equivalent of about $2 million.

8   Johnson would later become the father of Lyndon Baines Johnson.

9   Today, Fiesta is an enormous production, with over a hundred nonprofit

organizations staging events citywide. A queen and twenty-four duchesses, twelve from San Antonio and twelve from out of town, are chosen by the Order of the Alamo. Being part of the royal court is akin to a society debut for many young Texas women. The parade is still the only parade in the United States produced solely by women.

10   There was a lawsuit when Oscar Hammerstein Sr. sued the Shubert brothers, claiming Fields Theatre had a contract for the show. The Shuberts prevailed, and the show opened at the Lyric Theater.

11   There is no record of why that date was chosen—it would have been some six months after the convention.

12   The official DRT report on the Goliad convention was not published for a year after the fact; Adina separately published her faction's version of the events in the meantime, and word quickly spread about the ongoing conflict.

13   Clara also wrote the governor and the legislature, offering to remove the Hugo and Schmeltzer building at her own expense and suggesting the stones from the original barracks be used for a wall "covered with graceful vines." She asked architects to draw plans for a park enclosed by a low wall with arched Spanish gateways. Years later, in 1931, the state government did appropriate money to build a park but didn't have the funds to buy the commercial buildings south of the chapel. Clara bought the property for $60,000 and deeded it to the state.

14   They were probably referring to Grenet's additions to the building.

15   Adina's detailed account of this 1935 trip is among her papers in the DRT Library of the Alamo.

16   The creator of the original window is not known, although folklore credits a Spanish carpenter. The window, "Rosa's Window" or the "Rose Window," is said to be one of the finest examples of baroque architecture in the United States.

17   In Italian the phrase roughly translates as Heavenly Lagoon.

18   Not to be confused with Austin's Driskill Hotel, which was conceived and built by cattleman Jesse Driskill in 1886. Biographer Martha Anne Turner discounts this story because it betrays a lack of genteel behavior that would have been uncharacteristic of Clara. On the other hand, she was known as tempestuous and outspoken. It could have happened.

BIBLIOGRAPHIC ESSAY

———————•●•———————

Debra Winegarten amassed a collection of books, articles, photocopies, handwritten notes, and whatever else she found, in preparation for writing this book. In short, she created a mini-research library on the second Battle of the Alamo. When I began work on the manuscript, Cindy Huyser sent the entire collection to me—a box of books and two cartons of loose material, one of them a huge Amazon carton. The collection was a bit overwhelming, but invaluable, as I dug into the subject. These materials will eventually be in a Debra Winegarten archive in the library of Texas Woman's University in Denton, available to future researchers. Many of the photocopies, however, are undated and some offer no indication of a source. I suspect Debra knew their origin, but as other hands collected her papers, the organization was muddled; what was clear to Debra was foggy to me. When the information seemed accurate, I incorporated many of these sources in this text.

For my research I relied heavily on the Handbook of Texas Online which is always objective, well-researched, and concise.

As with any other subject, the Alamo presents the researcher the challenge of sifting the wheat from the chaff. The number of people with pet theories about everything from the original battle to Adina De Zavala and Clara Driscoll or even the current status of the Alamo far outweighs the objective scholarly treatment of the subject. It behooves one to read with a healthy bit of skepticism.

Readers wanting a general history of the Texas Revolution would do well to check the Texas State Historical Association at tshaonline.org/home. Material about the Alamo and the Spanish mission system fills several libraries. For this project, I relied on a few basic sources: the "Spanish Missions" entry by Robert E. Wright, O.M.I. at tshaonline.org gives a good overview of the mission system; and, also at tshaonline.org, the "Battle of the Alamo" entry by Stephen L. Hardin speaks specifically to the history of the Alamo.

Adina De Zavala published *History and Legends of the Alamo and Other Missions in and around San Antonio* in 1917. It has since been edited by Richard Flores and was reprinted by Arte Publico Press of Houston in 1996.

Frank Thompson's *The Alamo: A Cultural History* (Dallas: Taylor Trade Publishing, 2012) provides a good overview of not only Alamo history but the way the myth has permeated our lives today. Thompson, a lifelong fan and student of the Alamo, is a screenwriter by profession, and sometimes he seems more captivated by the image than the history. His discussion of Alamo movies is particularly helpful.

Following up on the movie treatment, I found two sites helpful: johnwayne-thealamo.com and imdb.com. The latter provides a cast of characters and reviews of the John Wayne movie.

For the current status of the Alamo, a complete if promotional overview of the restoration project is found at alamoplazaproject .com/AlamoPlazaRestorationProject.pdf. See also savethealamo.us/the-second-battle.

Although some journalists refer to the contemporary battle over the Alamo as the second battle, it is of course the third, with a skirmish in 2012 when the mother of then-mayor Julian Castro scorned the legend of battle. Paul Burka's account of that controversy can be found at texas monthly.com/burka-blog/the-second-battle-of-the-alamo-fox-news-vs -julian-castros-mom.

There is little written about the true second battle, but sources provide comprehensive information about the major participants. *Echoes from Women of the Alamo* by Gale Hamilton Shiffrin (San Antonio: AW Press, 1999) offers objective, factual, and balanced essays on both Adina De Zavala and Clara Driscoll and is, I found, the most reliable source.

Just as Clara Driscoll has gotten the most attention for saving the Alamo, she gets the lion's share of study. *Clara Driscoll: An American Tradition* by Martha Anne Turner (Austin: Madrona Press, 1979) is a detailed study of Driscoll's life but seemingly written to affirm her reputation and extoll her virtues. There is no mention of Adina De Zavala, and the reader must watch for a few factual errors and distractions such as exhaustive detail on the rivalry between FDR and John Nance Garner (Driscoll was a dedicated Democrat and her loyalties were torn by the split between the two men). The "Driscoll" entry in the Handbook of Texas Online is found at tshaonline.org/handbook/online/articles/fdr04.

The Woman's Collection at Texas Woman's University holds a typescript labeled, "Clara Driscoll: Savior of the Alamo," by Janelle D. Scott. This essay is the source for the assertion that Clara stayed in Spain during the Spanish-American War.

Want to know what Clara might have worn as Queen of the San Antonio Festival? Just for fun, check Nell Patteson's *Clara Driscoll, "Savior of the Alamo," Her Life Story*, A Paper Doll Book (Smiley, Texas: Smiley Originals, n.d.).

Because Driscoll's fiction reflects much of her values and attitudes, particularly toward Mexicans, it is interesting to read her three major published works: *In the Shadow of the Alamo* (Knickerbocker Press, New York, 1908); *The Girl of La Gloria* (G. P. Putnam's Sons / The Knickerbocker Press, New York, 1905); *Mexicana: A Mexican Comic Opera* by Raymond Hubbell and Clara Driscoll, 1906, from Stanford University Library Drama Collection, A NABU Public Document Reprint, 2003.

Beyond Shiffrin's work, there are almost no reliable overviews of the life and extraordinary accomplishments of Adina De Zavala. The Texas State Historical Association offers general biographical information about De Zavala and the Daughters of the Republic of Texas. In an article for *Southwestern Historical Quarterly* (January 1967), Robert L. Ables explored the significance of Adina's preservation work. A typescript of Ables's thesis is among the research materials compiled by Debra Winegarten.

Las Tejanas: 300 Years of History, by Teresa Palomo Acosta and Ruthe Winegarten, was helpful in studying De Zavala's relationship with her Spanish heritage and in countering the more extreme views of Richard Flores and Suzanne Seifert Cottraux.

Remembering the Alamo: Memory, Modernity, and the Master Symbol (Austin: University of Texas Press, 2002) opens with a long essay by Richard Flores, essentially protesting that the treatment of Mexicans seems rooted in earlier interpretations of the battle that paint it as a massacre with lily-white heroes and black-devil villains. Calling the Alamo a racist symbol, he develops an unsubstantiated theory that Adina De Zavala felt guilt over denying her Mexican heritage. His essay is to be read with extreme caution.

Suzanne Seifert Cottraux's iconoclastic master's thesis in history ("Mixed Identity: Collective Memory—Adina De Zavala and the Tejano Heritage that Wasn't," University of Texas at Arlington, May 2013) is a psychosocial study that focuses on the way issues of race and gender shaped Adina's life, although it does credit her historical work. Both Flores and Cottraux illustrate a tendency to bring twenty-first-century sensibilities to the interpretation of Adina's early-twentieth-century life.

Adina was an inveterate notetaker, journalist, scribbler, and she left behind a treasure trove of articles, notes, and papers to be found either at the Barker Center for American History on the campus of the University of Texas or in the archives of the University of the Incarnate Word in San Antonio. Other collections are found at the DRT headquarters, the archives at Texas Woman's University, and the University of Texas at Arlington.

Adina's journal of her 1935 trip to East Texas and western Louisiana, with Frances Donecker, is found in typescript form in her papers at the DRT Library.

Much background information on the Daughters of the Republic of Texas can be found in the book by Shiffrin and, to a lesser extent, in Turner's biography of Driscoll. *The Handbook of Texas Online* once again provides objective facts: tshaonline.org/handbook/online/articles/vnd03. For some light on Adina's work after she left the DRT, see tsha online.org/handbook/online/articles/vtt03. The site curiously talks of the Texas Historical and Landmark Association annual meetings in the present tense when they have been disbanded since the 1950s.

There is one novel loosely—very loosely—based on the second battle. The figure at the center of *Alamo Heights* by Scott Zesch blends features of Adina and Clara: Rose Herrera is passionate about preserving the Alamo, but more like Clara, she speeds around San Antonio in her Peerless tourer. She is not, however, a ranch heiress but the wife of an uptight conservative lawyer trying to overcome the social stigma of his Mexican heritage. The most authentic episode in the novel is Rose's occupation of the long barracks. For all its distortion of history, *Alamo Heights* is fun to read. The definitive novel of the second battle also remains to be written.

Additional suggestions for the serious student of the first Battle of the Alamo:

Entertainer Phil Collins, an Alamo collector heavily involved in the Alamo Plaza Project and author of *The Alamo and Beyond: A Collector's Journey*, leads off his choice of the five best Alamo books with Stephen L. Hardin's *Texian Iliad*, a scholarly study of the Texas Revolution and the Alamo battle. Others on the list are *Exodus from the Alamo* by Phillip Thomas Tucker, which Collins describes as a revisionist history; *The Illustrated Alamo 1836*, photographs of a scale model in a less-than-authentic desert setting—the model is on display in San Antonio; *The Alamo: An Illustrated History* by George Nelson, which Collins describes as a "must" for Alamo enthusiasts; and *An Altar for Their Sons* by Gary S. Zaboly, based on contemporary newspaper clippings.

Some titles that Collins left out: *The Alamo Story* by J. R. Edmondson, a general historical narrative; *Three Roads to the Alamo* by William C. Davis, biographies of Crockett, Travis, and Bowie; *13 Days to Glory* by Lon Tinkle, published in the mid-twentieth century and considered the definitive account of the battle, although new research has made it dated; *The Blood of Heroes* by James C. Donovan, a retelling by a talented storyteller, valuable for its extensive documentation as well.

INDEX

ABOUT THE AUTHOR

---•●•---

Judy Alter is the author of over a hundred books, fiction and nonfiction, for both adults and young adults. Her awards include the 2005 Owen Wister Award for Lifetime Achievement, Spur Awards from Western Writers of America, the Western Heritage (Wrangler) Award from the National Cowboy Museum and Hall of Fame, and a Best Juvenile of the Year Award from the Texas Institute of Letters. She was named one of the Outstanding Women of Fort Worth by the Mayor's Commission on the Status of Women in 1989 and was listed by *Dallas Morning News* (March 10, 1999) as one of a hundred women, past and present, who made their mark on Texas. She has been inducted into the Western Writers of America Hall of Fame and the Texas Literary Hall of Fame.

A novelist, Alter is the author of historical fiction about women in the American West. Novels include *Sundance, Butch and Me*; *Cherokee Rose*; *Jessie; Libbie; Mattie*; and *The Gilded Cage*. Alter's publications include cookbooks, a short story collection, and a critical biography of Texas novelist Elmer Kelton. In addition, she has written historical fiction and nonfiction for young-adult readers.

After an established career writing historical fiction and nonfiction, in 2011 Judy Alter turned her attention to contemporary cozy mysteries, writing three series set in Texas.

Alter was editor of TCU Press for five years and director from 1987 until 2011. She holds a PhD in English with a special interest in the literature of the American West from TCU, a MEd in English from Truman

University in Missouri, and a BA from the University of Chicago. She is a past president of Western Writers of America, former secretary-treasurer of the Texas Institute of Letters, and a member of Sisters in Crime. Find her online at http://wwwjudyalter.com; her blogs, judys-stew.blogspot.com and gourmetonahotplate.blogspot.com; also on Facebook, Twitter (@judyalter), and Amazon.

A native of Chicago, Alter has lived in Texas for over fifty years. She is the single parent of four now-grown children and the grandmother of seven. She lives in Fort Worth in a cottage she shares with her poodle/border collie, Sophie.